TO BE
Frank

TO BE

Frank

MEMORIES
OF AN
EXTRAORDINARY
LIFE

FRANK DYKE

EDITED BY JOAN SULLIVAN

1 Stamp's Lane, St. John's, NL, Canada, A1E 3C9
WWW.BREAKWATERBOOKS.COM

Library and Archives Canada Cataloguing in Publication
Dyke, Frank, 1922-
To be Frank : memories of an extraordinary life / Frank Dyke ; edited by Joan Sullivan.
ISBN 978-1-55081-383-8

1. Dyke, Frank, 1922-. 2. Newfoundland and Labrador--Biography.
3. World War, 1939-1945--Veterans--Newfoundland and Labrador--Biography.
4. Veterans--Newfoundland and Labrador--Biography. I. Title.

FC2177.1.D85A3 2012   971.8'05092   C2012-900919-9

We acknowledge the support of the Canada Council for the Arts which last year
invested $24.3 million in writing and publishing throughout Canada. We acknowledge the
Government of Canada through the Canada Book Fund and the Government of Newfoundland and Labrador through the Department of Tourism, Culture and
Recreation for our publishing activities.

PRINTED AND BOUND IN CANADA.

Canada Council   Conseil des Arts   Canadä   Newfoundland
for the Arts   du Canada   Labrador

Breakwater Books is committed to choosing papers and materials for our books that help
to protect our environment. To this end, this book is printed on a recycled paper that is
certified by the Forest Stewardship Council®.

Printed on Silva Enviro 100% post-consumer EcoLogo certified paper,
processed chlorine free and manufactured using biogas energy.

TO MY DAUGHTER,
EYDIE,
AND MY GRANDSON,
JOSHUA.

I enlisted in the 59th Heavy Newfoundland Regiment and served for nearly five years until the war ended in 1945. The history of World War II has been researched and written about by many others including highly regarded historians, so I am not attempting to encroach upon, or to duplicate anyone else's work. The same proviso applies to the Korean conflict, a pre-*Glasñost* Moscow, the swimming pool of the British Sudan Club in Khartoum, and the many other places and events that form this memoir. I am merely writing about my own personal experiences and, although some of the scenarios described may not be exactly as they happened, they are as I remember them.

PROLOGUE

It was 1940. Just months earlier, on September 3, 1939, Great Britain had declared war on Germany. I would soon turn 18, and, like many other adventure-seeking young Newfoundlanders, I was planning to travel to St. John's to enlist in the Armed Forces. My mother, Elizabeth Osmond, thought that I was being rather foolhardy to leave the safety of home to go to some foreign country where I might be putting myself in danger. Hadn't I already been snatched, by an act of divine intervention, from the jaws of death? As a very young child, I had fallen into an open well, where there was a rock, just high enough to keep my head above water until my older brother Max was able to yank me out. Surely my life had been spared for some higher purpose than traipsing off like this? She warned me to be careful. As I stood on the wharf in Frenchman's Cove, waiting for my transportation to St. John's, neither she nor I had any idea of the horrors and dangers that World War II would inflict on the world.

I was born in Port Union, Trinity Bay, June 9, 1922, but soon after my family moved to the west coast of Newfoundland. Growing up in Corner Brook, I always looked forward to summer vacations when school would be out and I could go to my most favourite place, the pilot station at Frenchman's Cove. The carefree, fun-filled life I lived there would probably seem very unsophisticated and boring to this present generation of teenagers whose lives revolve around computers, electronic games, TV, toys and gadgets. To me and to my friends, it was near perfection, and I still connect, on occasion, with people from that time in my life. We spent many summer days on the water using our mothers' used flour sacks to make sails for our dories, and we either sailed or rowed out to a favourable spot to set our lobster pots or salmon nets, or to just throw our hooks overboard to catch a few trout. On other lazy days, we swam or just horsed around to amuse ourselves. I don't remember our parents ever being overly concerned about our safety while we were hijinxing on the water. Days we stayed on land, we went berrypicking for raspberries and blueberries in Frenchman's Cove and for bakeapples on Governor's Island where we filled our stomachs and our buckets. I can still remember the smell of new mown hay as we spent many enjoyable summer days making hay and finally jumping it down in the barns of the local farmers.

Although Corner Brook was no metropolis in the 1930s and 40s, compared to Frenchman's Cove the lifestyle there was quite racy. When my family decided to spend some winters in Frenchman's Cove, I went to Corner Brook to attend school, boarding with family acquaintances there. Restrictions were usually placed on my activities during school nights, but I was still able to escape on a Friday or Saturday night to play in a band called the Brockway Brothers. I was all of 14 at that time. There were movies and other activities associated with an average-sized papermill town, with a population of approximately five to six thousand people, but Frenchman's Cove was always calling me when the school year ended. The lifestyle there was so relaxed and natural, as I suppose it was in most outports at that time. The pilot station was only about 30 or 40 feet from the water and, at night, with the bedroom windows wide open and the curtains billowing in the breezes, we could hear the soothing sounds of the waves breaking on the beach. The smell of the ocean from the salty sea breezes blowing in from York Harbour, and the floating beds of kelp rolling on to the shore, are still a part of my childhood memories. In those days, most residents of Frenchman's Cove, in fact, people all over the Bay of Islands, had gardens and grew their own vegetables. In Frenchman's Cove, the main source of fertilization was kelp in addition to cattle manure and, at times, a good ground covering of caplin and herring. The end results were crops of excellent produce equal to or surpassing some of the organic produce so highly promoted today. There were no washing machines or clothes dryers, at least in my little corner of the world, in the 1930s and early 40s. Consequently, long lines of hand-washed clothes hanging out to dry were a part of every household. To this day, I still appreciate the smell of line-dried clothes. As was the case in most outports in earlier years, doors were seldom locked, and neighbours were free to drop in whenever they felt like doing so, perhaps to listen to the old Atwater Kent radio at the pilot station or just for a chat. Sometimes, one had to put out the cat, which seems like an insensitive thing to do today, then stoke up the stove and make the necessary preparations for bed, before some reluctant visitors took the hint and departed for their own homes. All in all though, the lifestyle suited me just fine. It was certainly preferable to some places I've lived in recent years when doors and windows had to be locked and sometimes barricaded, both day and night, and where we scarcely recognized our neighbours.

My father, Captain Nathan Dyke, was Harbour Pilot for foreign ships coming into the Bay of Islands to dock in Corner Brook and, consequently, he divided his time between Frenchman's Cove and Corner Brook. A call on our ancient phone at Frenchman's Cove would summon him with three long and three short rings when a ship was approaching the lighthouse at the entrance to the Bay of Islands, usually at South Head. The pilot boat would transport him to the waiting ship. It always fascinated me that a man of his girth could so easily and nimbly climb the rope ladder to board these huge vessels, sometimes in strong winds and in inclement weather. A previous pilot had both of his legs severed when a wave threw the pilot boat against the side of the ship while he was climbing up the rope ladder attempting to board the vessel. Since insurance companies dictated that a certified and experienced Harbour Pilot be in control of an incoming or outgoing ship, my father would direct the helmsmen as to the course to be steered, and he did this with never a mishap. It never ceases to amuse me that when he acquired his first automobile, a shiny green and white 1953 Chevy Belair, and began to drive at the age of 65, he never did master the art of parallel parking. Actually, he could hardly depart the dock without running into anything that seemed to be in his path, even a heavy crane on one occasion. His new vehicle was soon dented and scratched and was often missing a hubcap or a fender, which he inevitably blamed on someone else's careless driving. It is remarkable that he was so adept at handling a 21,000-ton ship, like the tourist liner *Volendam* or the SS *Franconia*, but could not safely steer an automobile. My father, widely referred to as The Skipper, and well known all over the Bay of Islands as a competent seaman, was, as a driver, announced by such kidding remarks as: "Clear the roadways, Captain Dyke is coming."

I remember my Dad would smoke and hold his cigarettes right close up to his mouth with his two fingers pressed up against his lips. He never inhaled but would take a puff, blow it out immediately, and in a cloud of smoke would advise me, "Frank, my son, don't ever take up smoking. I only do it because I get the cigarettes off the ship for free." He was not ever worried about having his bottles of rum confiscated because he always remembered to bring one for the customs officer on duty.

In January 1923, the *Twillingate Sun* and *Weekly Advertiser* reported the following story:

> January 20, 1923, News from Port Union. Several men of Port Union were presented with certificates of recognition for their bravery from Mr. Coaker for their great courage and persistence in their efforts to quell the fire on the ship *Port Union* which was recently destroyed at that place. One Nathan Dyke, at the risk of being drowned, crawled over the boards laid on the slob and snow, and reached the burning ship with a rope, which enabled the fire fighters to haul a dory through the slob. After three hours of hard work, their efforts proved in vain and the ship had to be abandoned to the flames.

I assume there was no loss of life and, also, that the men's bravery was their own and that they didn't get it from Mr. Coaker as the article suggests.

In 1937, my father received a call from the lighthouse keeper at South Head. Two ships identifying themselves as United States warships the USS *Tuscaloosa* and the USS *Lang* were requesting the services of a Harbour Pilot as they wished to enter the Bay of Islands. I accompanied my father on the pilot boat to Lark Harbour where the cruisers were hove to. Imagine my father's surprise when he boarded the ship and came face to face with American President Franklin Delano Roosevelt. He and his entourage were in Newfoundland for a salmon fishing adventure on the Humber River.

It was perhaps my father who instilled in me a sense of adventure as he had travelled far in his earlier years as a merchant seaman. In any event, it was my father's interaction with the ships coming into the Bay of Islands that made it possible for me to spend summers in Frenchman's Cove at the pilot station, and eventually for my leaving from that place to participate in World War II.

PART ONE

It was a warm Newfoundland morning, but foggy and rainy, when I, with my backpack of personal belongings and my trusty mandolin, headed down to the pilot's wharf in Frenchman's Cove. Here I boarded the *Ada M. Westhaver*, a 200-ton coastal schooner owned and captained by my father's good friend, Captain Job Blackwood. The schooner was a fore-and-after carrying a mainsail, foresail, a jumbo and a jib. Some people called such schooners Jack boats (similar to the Grand Bank fishing vessel). I considered myself most fortunate to have this means of transportation to St. John's, my intended place of enlistment. At that time, almost 70 years ago, unless one lived on or near the railway line, travelling to St. John's could be something of an ordeal. Boats were widely used in summer, but at other times of the year people living in coastal areas were dependent on dog teams or on horse and sleigh to travel anywhere.

As we departed Frenchman's Cove aboard the *Westhaver*, I was looking forward to the northern route trip. The schooner's crew was made up of five men, plus the Captain's son, John, and me along as passengers. As we headed out the Bay of Islands and turned north, the winds picked up and we encountered heavy rain and dense fog but, in spite of the terrible weather, our spirits remained high. By mid-afternoon the fog had lifted and the rain had stopped but the winds remained strong and the conditions were then perfect for smooth sailing.

And for poetry, it seems, as I wrote the following:

> Here I am at age eighteen,
> In the best place for sailing t'would seem,
> Sailing cross the mouth of White Bay,
> With a northern on her beam.

During our entire trip, beginning at the Bay of Islands, we encountered many hours of dense fog but, in spite of the fact that Captain Job was often unable to see land, his basic instruments and his skills were sufficient for the task. He had an ancient hand-operated foghorn that he pointed toward where he presumed the land was, pumped it a few times and waited for the echo. To determine the schooner's speed, Captain Job used a short piece of two-by-four on a rope which he threw off at the bow and which he trailed back tothe schooner's stern. Of course, his regional charts were also helpful when the fog happened to lift and when we were navigating around difficult areas like Notre Dame Bay which had a proliferation of islands of various sizes. Along the route, it was necessary to replenish our fresh water supply and this we did at Twillingate. I recall asking Captain Job how hecould navigate so skillfully and he said, "I can smell the land, Frank Boy, I can smell the land." I guess that was not far from the truth as, in many cases, that seemed to be the only way he did it during nighttime sailing, though the many lighthouses that dotted the coastline provided us with a greater sense of security.

Other than the problems caused by the winds, which had picked up to gale-force strength after we crossed White Bay, making it necessary to double-reef the mainsail and foresail for most of the way to St. John's, our trip was pretty much routine. On one occasion, Captain Job decided to give me something to do as he had not been too impressed with my mandolin playing, mostly jigs and other popular Newfoundland music. He considered it a distraction for the crew and a waste of valuable time, so he decided that John and I should do some painting of the decks. John became a doctor in later life and seemed, even at that time, to be dedicated to whatever task he was assigned. After a couple of hours, Captain came to check on our progress. He took one disgusted look at my bespattered clothes and body and said, "For the love of Mike, put down the paintbrush Frankie, and go back to your gawl-durn madaloop." He left me to my own pursuits from that time on until we finally arrived in St. John's and tied up at one of the old finger-jetties at Harvey & Company wharf. As usual, St. John's was enshrouded in fog as I made my way to 100 Duckworth Street, my Uncle Nathan Osmond's residence. My movements, for the few days that I spent there, were rather restricted. My Aunt Louie, a staunch Salvationist (Salvation Army member), was even appalled that I would defile the Lord's Day by pressing my pants. When she discovered my sinful act, she took away the ironing board, and I accompanied her to church with only one pressed pant leg.

In July 1942, the Newfoundland Department of Defence ordered the Newfoundland Militia to help recruit and train reinforcements for two overseas regiments of the British Royal

Artillery composed of Newfoundlanders. I was assigned to the "59th Heavy," one of the "166th Field Artillery Regiments." The first 100 recruits departed for Britain in September 1942, after completing the 12-week training course at Shamrock Field in St. John's. When enough recruits to complete a draft had finished training, we boarded the SS *Fort Amherst*, a passenger liner en route to Halifax, Nova Scotia.

The first day out of St. John's we were escorted by an RCAF Hudson Bomber. That day, we made our first kill when about halfway through the trip, the alarm sounded. We donned our life jackets and proceeded to the side for further action. We saw that the Hudson Bomber had swooped down over the water ahead of us, and the crew, thinking they detected one of the German submarines known to be patrolling that area, dropped a depth charge. A poor 50- to 60-foot sperm whale floated to the surface. Without further consequence, we proceeded on to dock in Halifax at Pier 21. The next day, we boarded the SS *Louis Pasteur*, a 29,253-ton troop ship. She was 212.4 metres long and 26.8 metres wide. The *Louis Pasteur* then went on to join the large convoy of ships at Bedford.

Already on board were the Governor General's Foot Guards and an Infantry Regiment out of Ottawa, 1,000 Polish troops, a large attachment of Royal Canadian Air Force (RCAF) personnel, and a number of Canadian nurses. We were each given a lifejacket, a hammock and a slip of paper indicating the location of our sleeping accommodations. As we proceeded down – one, two, three, four, five decks – I began to think, if we got torpedoed, and there was a better than average chance that we might, with approximately three to four thousand troops on board, it would be quite a panic to get up to the main deck with only four available stairways. During the course of the day, however, my attention was drawn to a notice posted on the bulletin board which requested that personnel familiar with machine guns report to the Regulation Petty Officer (RPO). Subsequently, I went to his office and informed him that I had knowledge of the Lewis machine gun (a weapon I was eventually able to strip and reassemble in less than one minute) having received some instruction and opportunities to fire one while at Shamrock Field. I was taken to the bridge area and checked out on the twin-mounted guns and, with another soldier on the port side of the ship, moved up to the bridge to be on-duty machine gunners. With this assignment, we were able to escape our bed accommodations in the bowels of the ship and to sleep on a heap of life jackets and sometimes, when we were able to do so secretly, in one of the life boats for a touch of luxury. This offered me some relief in case we were torpedoed, and the brisk September air was a luxury for us as we made our way across the Atlantic. (And, as it happened, the Lewis machine guns were not activated during the convoy's crossing as there was no enemy aircraft activity. We were out of range of the German aircraft.)

The swiftness of the convoy was limited to the pace of the slowest ship, in this case, the SS *Phillip T. Dodge*, top speed six knots. I have no idea how large the convoy was except to say it was massive. During the 3,000-mile crossing, over what had become the most dangerous expanse of ocean in the world, we lost somewhere around 17 ships.

The German High Command, under the leadership of Nazi Commander, Karl Donitz, had instituted a new strategy of submarine warfare called *Rudel*. *Rudel* translates best as a "pack" (as of animals) and has become known in English as "wolf pack" (*Wolfsrudel*), a more accurately metaphoric, but not literal, interpretation. Several groups of submarines, U-boats, would lay submerged in the path of the convoy waiting to attack at the most opportune times for them, when it was possible to surface in the centre of the moving convoy. The convoy was arranged in "line ahead" formation with the commodore ship being in the centre. The remainder of the convoy was organized in strategic formation, with high octane gas and explosives on the outside, then all sorts of ammunition, aircraft, guns, tanks and general cargo including food and the troops. Unfortunately, although many attacks were foiled by the counteraction of Canadian and British destroyers and corvettes (small ships) and, in some cases, by American warships that were in the area, the wolf pack was successful in destroying too many lives and several hundreds of thousands of tons of shipping over the course of that journey. One of my most vivid and painful memories is that of seeing a huge tanker on fire, and watching as men plunged from the burning vessel into the equally fiery sea, which was no alternative at all.

For the remaining time of our crossing, our convoy maintained its zigzag across the Atlantic. This practice was implemented ostensibly to provide a changing and moving target for the ever-present U-boats and proved to be, in spite of our losses, an effective ruse. I can't recall how long it took us to cross, but as we neared the Irish Sea, our ship, the *Louis Pasteur*, left the convoy, and at full speed, over 26 knots, headed for our ultimate destination, Greenock on the River Clyde in Scotland, which flows through the major city of Glasgow. As we approached the entrance to the river, we saw a huge ship anchored in midstream that was painted battleship grey and had an enormous hole in her port bow at water level. Several years after the war was over, we learned that the ship was the *Queen Mary* and that the damage had occurred somewhere in the North Atlantic when a Royal Navy escort cruiser got its directions confused and zigged when it should have zagged, running into her. After repairs were made, the *Queen Mary* continued to transport hundreds of thousands of troops to Europe from the US and, later, returning the veterans after the war, always unescorted.

The *Louis Pasteur* anchored in the River Clyde, and a steam-propelled paddle-wheeler transported all troops to dockside. From there, we were taken by buses to the railway station at Greenock and immediately, by train, to Ashford in Kent, England. Military transport then delivered the troops to their designated batteries. I was going to Patterson's Farm, the location of 22 Battery and a part of the 59th Newfoundland Regiment. I remained there for several months of training pertaining to the signals operations of heavy artillery. This continued as we moved to Mabledon Park, a small government area located between Tonbridge and Tumbridge Wells. We also became actively involved in military sports to build up our physiques and to occupy our spare time while awaiting our move to the continent and active service. Sometime later, for reasons un-known, we were moved to Bourne Grange, Hadlow, a distance of only a few miles but closer to London. We were well received by the local people, but not so much so by the enemy. Hitler's *Luftwaffe* kept deploying their V-1 bombs with their 1,000-pound warheads over us at regular intervals from launching sites in Belgium. These were unmanned and carried only enough fuel to take them to southern England, including and especially London, where they exploded upon impact. When the V-1s were first used, no one could stop them. Then the British began to use their fastest planes, the Mosquito Fighter bombers, flying side-by-side with them and nudging them out into the Channel to crash there instead of on land.

The Germans would fire these every five minutes. London was an important target for the enemy because, at this time, all the counties of southeastern England were being developed into a gigantic holding area for all imaginable types of weaponry – tanks, guns, ammunition, vehicles, etc., in preparation for the inevitable invasion of Normandy in northern France. On several occasions, because of our proximity to the English Channel, we witnessed firsthand much of the action taking place both in the air and on the sea in that area – dog fights involving the RAF Spitfires and Hurricanes and the Germans' fighter planes, ME109s and FW190s in the Channel and battles between the German EBoats (Enemy Boat, a fast torpedo craft) and the British MGBs (motor gun boats).

While we were still in a holding position and, since we were only a short train ride from London, we took advantage of our free weekend passes to go there. We often found lodging at the Newfoundland Caribou Club, located on Trafalgar Square and known as the best club in London, or at The Salvation Army Red Shield Club. It was exciting to see the sights of London, but devastating to observe all the damage that had been done by the days, nights and weeks of endless bombing. Surprisingly enough, Trafalgar Square escaped the onslaught almost unscathed and, even more surprising, up until that time, Buckingham Palace had been hit only once. During one German air raid, I, being caught out somewhere in the heart of the city, was directed by a London bobby to the deep shelter, several hundred steps down to Holborn-Kingsway tramway (subway) station. This underground shelter was similar to a small village with air raid wardens, first aid people, people serving food and tea – usually The Salvation Army – and with bunks to accommodate hundreds of people. Above, we could hear the bombs falling and feel the earth shaking. These assaults continued on London, and other selected targets over the United Kingdom, night after night for weeks on end until one began to wonder how there could be anything left to strike. After the Americans joined the war, they built airfields all over central England and from there they launched incessant air raids on selected targets all over Europe, including the Ploesti oilfields in Romania, ball-bearing factories in Schweinfurt, Germany, and other Nazi strongholds. The Americans attacked by day and the RAF by night.

Not all of our free weekend passes were spent in London. On other occasions, we went to Manchester, England, or to Glasgow, Scotland – the latter being a popular place for Newfoundlanders, mostly because of the friendliness of the Scottish people. We were happy to find ourselves in Glasgow on January 25, 1943, and to be able to attend the Robert Burns Night Celebrations and Dance. The effort made by the people to ensure that the troops had a memorable time was much appreciated. It was impossible to spend money there because no one would let us. A rollicking song, sung with great gusto, remains in my mind:

> I belong to Glasgow, dear old Glasgow town
> What's the matter with Glasgow
> for it's going round and round
> I'm only a common old working chap
> as anyone here can see

But when I get a couple of drinks on a Saturday,
Glasgow belongs to me

The Glasgow brogue made it extra special.

While in the Glasgow area, I took a side trip to Paisley, some thirty miles away, to visit a Newfoundland friend, Ernie May. While waiting for his work day to end, I dropped into a pub where I was greeted cordially, but when I went down to Ernie's later that evening and told him where I had been, he said, "What, you were where?!" He went on to explain to me that I had been in the hangout of the toughest gang in Scotland – the Razor Gang. Their insignia was a straight razor sewn into the visor of their caps, yet all they wanted to do to me was to buy me a drink. Perhaps they appreciated Newfoundland soldiers!

In the midst of all the carnage taking place in England during the fall of 1942, our stays in London continued to provide entertainment in the form of dances and parties. Covent Garden, in Central London, had been converted from an opera house to a dance pavilion, and it could accommodate up to 3,000 people and it had two alternating dance bands, one of which, the Ivy Benson Band, was made up entirely of female musicians. It was a fine place for dances providing you were not a jitterbugger ("No Jitterbugging Permitted!") and a popular place for military personnel to socialize, get a break from the rigours of training in preparation for war, and to just generally unwind. There were other activities ongoing and, on one occasion, I remember being invited to the Lord Mayor's Mansion House in London for an honorary dinner given for Lieutenant General Sir Adrian Carton de Wiart. Each of the Colonies of the British Empire was represented by a member of the three branches of the military. For Newfoundland, Flight Lieutenant Sandy Candow represented the Royal Air Force (RAF), I represented the Royal Artillery/Army, and a sailor, best left unnamed as he completely flubbed all protocol, represented the Navy.

During one of our weekend passes to London, we were invited to 58 Victoria Street where the Newfoundland Trade Commissioner hosted and provided us with a typical New-foundland meal of fish and brewis. It was a great reminder of home, even though some of us were great fish but not brewis fans. It was at this dinner that we were introduced to Margot Davies, daughter of the Trade Commissioner. She was the social director and general liaison person between the Trade Commission and the Newfoundland Troops, providing us with many of the comforts of home including warm clothing – socks, mitts and sweaters – most of which had been hand knit by Newfoundland women doing their part for the war effort. The Trade Commission also ensured that the flow of incoming and outgoing mail proceeded smoothly. For her many unselfish efforts on our behalf, Margot Davies was awarded the Member of the British Empire Award (MBE) in 1944. Starting in 1941 she also hosted the BBC's *Calling to Newfoundland from Britain* radio program. It was aired every Sunday night and was very popular with Newfoundlanders, especially those who had relatives and friends serving in the British military.

Our weekend passes to London, and to other surrounding areas, were not always about fun and relaxation. They were often, for a certain faction of the regiment, an opportunity to engage in some of the most crude and downright embarrassing conduct imaginable. To say that this particular element was rude and rambunctious is an understatement – their main agenda seemed to be to cause as much havoc and chaos as possible, wherever they happened to be. They often interrupted speakers at events, to such an extent that they had to be removed by police. At one, Ms. Davies was rudely shouted down and she, being very gracious, attributed their atrocious behaviour to their youth, their being far away from their homes and loved ones for the first time, and to their being on the verge of going to war – they were merely sowing their wild oats. A behavioural analyst might have looked for a deeper cause to explain the bad behaviour – some have postulated that it might have been a form of retaliation for the deplorable acts inflicted upon the inhabitants of Newfoundland by the British Empire when they dispatched the fishing admirals to our shores to plunder the fishing industry. For almost five hundred years the fishing admirals together with the St. John's merchants became quite well-off on the backs of the Newfoundland fisherman. While many of the merchants lived in mansions, compared to the dwellings of regular people at the time, and sent their children off to school in England, and while the fishing admirals spent their winters in relative luxury in England, the Newfoundland fisherman struggled to survive, and in some cases starved to death, between fishing seasons. Newfoundlanders were sup-posed to be loyal to the British Empire and to defend its flag and reigning monarch in spite of the harsh treatment they had received from the mother country. Some would say, and not without cause, that Newfoundlanders who went to fight in the war certainly did not do it out of love for Great Britain but rather for the larger and greater cause.

While we were waiting to go into battle, there was a multitude of regiments made up of Irish, Scottish and English all over the southern part of England just biding time until D-Day. In any event, it seemed that if the "Fighting Newfoundlanders" couldn't pick a quarrel with their British, Scottish or Irish counterparts, they fought amongst themselves without just cause but with great fervour, which kind of dispels the notion that they were doing it for retaliation. They would even get into fights with their best friends and beat the living daylights out of them and be buddies with them again shortly afterwards.

Some things that took place were regarded as harmless pranks by those who instigated them, but ransacking and destroying furniture and other property, resulting in the banning of all Newfoundland regimental personnel from all but two pubs, the Lord High Admiral and The Surprise, could hardly be considered mere jokes. There was a lovely club called the Chandos, just around the corner in Trafalgar Square, where we used to go get delicious and rare sandwiches. That treat was ruined by the hooliganism.

One night the police apprehended a gang of regimental hoodlums attempting to remove a piano from the Caribou Club. I remember another time, under cover of darkness during an air raid, an officer who was particularly despised by many members of our unit was assaulted with a brick to the side of his head. Of course, under the circumstances, it was impossible to apprehend the deranged soldier who perpetrated this despicable act. Another evening at a club, a drunken sailor picked up a huge bucket of sand from a fire-fighting area and, standing on the landing of the second floor, threw it in the direction of the head of the lady at the front desk, missing her by inches. Such juvenile behaviour did nothing to endear Newfoundlanders to the local population. No publication that I am aware of ever addressed this aspect of rampant thuggery and it was, for the most part, ignored or excused by regimental authority. However, I witnessed it first hand and found it to be most disgusting. But, in spite of this unsavoury element, the Newfoundland service men, whether Army, Navy or Air Force, earned and maintained a stellar reputation throughout World War II as they had also done in World War I and would do during the Korean conflicts.

Our training, which had begun upon our arrival in the British Isles, continued out of our regimental headquarters in Hilden-borough. Incidentally, we Newfoundlanders were not considered to be serving overseas after going to England because, at that time, we were still a part of the British Empire. Conversely, Canadians were overseas when they came to serve in Gander or St. John's and, of course, when they went to England.

Part of this while we were still stationed in England involved, among other things, shooting exercises carried out on the wide open spaces of Brecon Barrens, Wales, the only area capable of accommodating our big guns. Because of my training, I was dispatched for signals courses to Redford Barracks in Edinborough, Scotland, and to New Romney in Kent where I took the Forward Observation Officer course (FOO). Those in other categories went to various other places.

During the course of our recreational experiences and while still at Ashford in Wales, one of the most popular activities, at least for me, was boxing. This included battery, inter-battery and regimental bouts, with varying degrees of boxing expertise and success or lack thereof. Although I am unable to confirm it personally, I was given to understand that one particularly well-accomplished boxer, who also happened to be the regimental sergeant major, used his considerable boxing skills to administer reprimands to soldiers being held for various crimes in Regimental Headquarters cells. It is said that he used 16-ounce gloves because they were very heavily padded and unlikely to mark his opponent. Thus, he could inflict the most effective punishment in the most invisible manner. Unfortunately for him, on one occasion, his method of sadistic chastisement backfired as his opponent turned out to be a street fighter from St. John's who was not overly intimidated by the oversized gloves or by their user. He wore his Army boots instead of gym shoes, and he was not hesitant about using his feet instead of his hands to overpower his opponent. After that, a substitute for the regimental sergeant major administered the appropriate discipline.

I must mention here that while in Ashford, during the course of a guard inspection, I was selected to receive what was known as the Stickman Award. This was given to the best turned out member of the guard – spiffy uniform, polished shoes, clean-shaven, shiny gun, etc. Although this was hardly comparable to any prestigious award like the Victoria Cross, it was to me, and to anyone else receiving it, a big deal. After all, my award resulted in my being excused from guard duty for 24 hours!

The holding pattern for the 59th Heavy Artillery Unit remained in place, and the troops of the various batteries continued to perform the mundane tasks necessary for the preparation for enemy combat. An interesting aspect of our training was to plan and execute battles to simulate what we would most certainly encounter once we faced the enemy on European soil. Other branches of the military also engaged in this type of training.

In 1944, from our station near London, we were only able to watch the bombing of the city by the German *Luftwaffe*. Then, somewhere in the midst of all the turmoil, around the end of April, when spring had arrived and everything was beginning to blossom in Southern England, we were summoned on a muster parade where we were told, in no uncertain terms, to divest ourselves of *all* personal belongings. Consequently, the second hand stores in the area around Hudlow, Tonbridge, and Tunbridge Wells became well-stocked and, because many goods were in short supply at this time, many people benefited from our significant loss – a good thing in that respect. Shortly thereafter, we were told to prepare for move out. We manned our vehicles and, together with our equipment and troops, headed north through London. Our 17-mile-long convoy was comprised of 16 heavy guns and their scammels together with the associated trucks carrying troops, weapons, ammunition and wireless radio trucks. We drove at 20 miles per hour, the maximum speed at which our guns could travel. It thus took us a considerable amount of time to move the relatively short distance from Kent to the small English fishing village of Sea Houses on the Scottish/English border. Sea Houses' only claim to fame was that of being home to Bamburg Castle on Holy Island. Some people believed this castle to be haunted. The "haunters" must have vacated the premises when they got wind of the Newfoundlanders' impending arrival, because we never spotted a "one of 'em."

As we passed through London, in the early hours of the morning, we saw lots of evidence of heavy bombing all along our route. Very few people were out and about as, to them, we were probably just another convoy passing through, and they already had plenty of their own problems with which to contend. We were told nothing about the reason for travelling north, what we would be doing there, nor how long we would be staying. It turned out we were there for approximately six weeks. We did little of any consequence during this period of time, so some of the more adventuresome amongst us made use of their leisure time to do some carousing and, as they described it, skirt-chasing. They even suggested they had shown some interest in the Scottish regiments decked out in their kilts. After all, it was only natural that Newfoundlanders, seeing a person in a kilt, would think – woman. (In the 1960s, while serving with the RCAF and stationed in France, I wore a kilt myself, as a member of the *One Fighter Wing Pipe and Drum Band*. We travelled extensively throughout the area and attracted huge crowds wherever we went. I assume the attention displayed by the European people was because of the music provided by the bagpipes and drums and not by the spectacle of a bunch of men in tartans, feather bonnets and kilts. The Germans referred to the band as "Dudelzaken." I don't know if that was a complementary name or not, but I can say that we were an extremely popular band.)

Once we arrived in Sea Houses, apart from firing practice rounds from our big guns out to sea, our stay was non-productive. Finally, we were given the order to mount up in preparation for our move to the south, and this was over the same route we had taken to drive north to our present location. When inquiries were made into the logic of this procedure, the response was, "You do not need to know." We did appreciate the fact, though, that this twice-travelled route covered the most scenic part of England, the Cotswolds. Because we were moving at such a slow speed, we were privileged to have the time and the opportunity to enjoy something beautiful before becoming involved in some of the horrific scenes which, unfortunately, were coming up on our horizon.

We passed through London and again we were able to view some of the remaining landmarks of the city like Trafalgar

Square, Nelson's monument, Buckingham Palace, the Caribou Club and others, and to be shocked at the devastation the German bombings had caused. Several V-1 unmanned bombs dropped and exploded in the vicinity of our convoy as we went by. Within a couple of hours, outside of London, we found ourselves in Worthing, a very popular seaside resort in brighter better days. This was one of the points of assembly for thousands of troops and their equipment, from all branches of the military, in preparation for the Channel crossing into the war zone of Normandy, France. When all was in readiness, we proceeded to Gosport, our embarkation point, where we were assigned to our designated landing craft. The big Landing Ship Tank (LST) was assigned to regimental headquarters personnel under the Lieutenant Colonel. The troops of the four batteries were designated to other landing craft. Being a member of the signals attachment, I went to United States Navy (USN) LST-494. Sleeping accommodations were non-existent and we slept, or tried to sleep, wherever we could find a space to lie down. In my case, that was in the radio truck. As for food, after our steady diet of cold rations, we were overjoyed to be able to partake of American food which, as is typical of Americans, they happily shared with us. We ate chicken, mashed potatoes, ice-cream, coffee and other such delicacies.

Speaking only for myself I can say that after what we had already witnessed in England, in the approximate ten hours that it took for us to cross the Channel I was, to say the very least, filled with apprehension about what was undoubtedly awaiting us on the continent. The time was ample for me to contemplate various aspects of our journey thus far, from our departure point in Newfoundland to our present position in the English

Channel. For instance, why had we been so long in England? In later years, I found out from a war historian in Ottawa that it was a matter of space, or lack thereof, available to the British/Canadian command. There was a preponderance of equipment and troops which filled, almost to capacity, the land area covered by Juneau, Sword and Gold Beaches on the Northern Coast of France. As forward movement liberated more territory, space became available to accommodate the 59th Newfoundland Heavy Regiment and we were now in the process of moving in.

As one can imagine, heavy traffic was always a part of the Channel scenario. During this crossing, with naval craft going in both directions, and numerous civilian shipping craft carrying out their normal trade, even in wartime still travelling through the north and south routes, the Channel was a beehive of activity. Previously, the shipping lanes had been under attack by German aircraft, but that was no longer a threat because of the dominance of the Royal Air Force in that area. Approaching the beaches of Normandy, the noises of the heavy guns continued to increase in intensity and, much too soon, we would be within their range. Of course, Naval craft were patrolling the shoreline from Utah (American) Beach to Gold (British) Beach and these provided us with a sense of security, at least for the time being. Even as our crafts touched the beach, the Royal Navy's HMS *Rodney* opened fire directly over our heads with a full-broadside of 16-inch guns firing 1,000-pound shells at an inland target. Near about noon, and before the landing craft was fully beached, my mother's caution of not putting myself in danger resonated in my mind. I felt like Henry Wadsworth Longfellow, in his poem "Day is Done":

The day is done, and the darkness
Falls from the wings of Night,
As a feather is wafted downward
From an eagle in his flight.

I see the lights of the village
Gleam through the rain and the mist,
And a feeling of sadness comes o'er me
That my soul cannot resist...

The worst was yet to come.

A little comic relief to kick off our operation began near the beach and involved a young soldier from St. John's who was determined to be the first Newfoundlander ashore on the beaches of Normandy. As the ramp from the landing craft was lowered, he started up his motorcycle and roared off the ramp into what he believed to be only a few inches of water. Unfortunately, the ramp was resting on a sandbar and the depth of the water between the sandbar and the beach was more like several feet. He was pulled out amid much laughter from his rescuers and the onlookers. He was probably feeling a little embarrassment at his plan having gone awry. After all, he was no ordinary soldier, he was a lieutenant!

By mid-May of 1944, it was reported that approximately a half million obstacles covered the area of the five beaches of Normandy. This vast number had been placed there by the Germans under the leadership of Field Marshall Erwin Rommel, who was also known as the Desert Fox because of his skill and intelligence in planning and strategy in the North African tank warfare. Rommel had said, "If we don't manage to throw them back at once, the invasion will succeed." He believed that the thousands of all types of mines, the barbed wire and the thousands of wood and metal objects would be very effective, and would prove to be a great deterrent to the allied forces attempting to land on the beaches. Although the British/Canadian Special Forces (engineers) had successfully defused and destroyed a vast number of these obstructions before the D-Day Landing, there was still plenty of evidence of their presence when we came ashore on July 5, 1944. Rommel's tactic very nearly paid off for the Germans. I have heard that, even with the large number of obstructions that had been diffused or destroyed, the average lifespan for someone landing on the beaches during D-Day was ten minutes. It is little wonder that so many had died in the landing and, to our horror, their bodies lay strewn all over the landscape. We were able to observe Army Engineers called Sappers engaged in the removal of what remained. We also saw, as we landed and pro-ceeded along the beach, a group of men in uniform and, upon closer surveillance, we noticed that the group was made up of rather elderly, or a least older, men than one would not expect to see in a war zone. They were wearing British Army uniforms and their shoulder insignia indicated that they belonged to the Pioneer Corps. True patriots, in spite of their less than robust health and their age, with some using canes and even a few being on crutches, they were determined to put forth their best efforts to aid in the allies' cause. They seemed to be engaged in all types of activities, doing whatever work needed to be done: building shelters, laying heavy wire mesh runways for the fighter aircraft that were landing there, digging slit trenches, operating generators and an infinite number of other tasks.

The Landing Crafts (four of the smaller ones) beached, unloaded, and we removed the waterproofing which had protected the sensitive equipment, especially the air-intake system, during the Channel crossing. The big LST and the LCTs beached and our regiments, along with the other personnel, equipment and vehicles on board, were directed to a designated area for dispersal. A number of regimental officers had gone to France as an advance party. They met us at the reception area where we landed and directed us to our battery positions. I was going to Battery 22. Incidentally, the Germans were several miles inland at this time having been forced to retreat to the Caen area by the Canadian and British Forces who were in that sector of Juno Beach.

When I consider all the horrendous noises produced by our guns together with those of the German 88s and of all of the weaponry of combat, I marvel that any of us, who were associated with the 59th Newfoundland Heavy Artillery Unit, have any hearing left at all, considering that we were never privy to the benefit of earplugs. Even the youngest of us are now in the late years of our lives, and most of us have been plagued with some degree of hearing impairment including tinnitus for most of our adulthood.

In convoy formation, our trucks, called scammels, towed our guns inland a few miles from the coast where our gun area had already been assigned. Our big guns were called 72 Gun Howitzers and were capable of firing 202-pound shells for a distance of 16,900 yards. A single gun weighed 101 tons, was 254 feet long, 9 feet wide and 43 feet high. It was capable of doing a great deal of damage upon impact.

En route from our landing area to the concentration location where we were now assembled, we were stunned at the scenes before us. Even after all we had experienced in England with the relentless bombings, we found it difficult to fully comprehend what we were seeing. All around us were demolished churches, shops, houses, farms, destroyed farmland and dead farm animals. As well, there were burned-out vehicles, tanks, lorries and concrete bunkers with heaps of rubble and mass devastation everywhere. The stench of death from lifeless and decaying bodies, which had assaulted our senses from the time we first landed on the beaches, still permeated the air. It dissipated somewhat as we went inland, but we were shocked to see the many crude graves, and sometimes bodies of those buried in the shallowest of graves, just below the surface, awaiting proper burial, we could only hope. A lot of this carnage had been caused by the allies in their mission to dislodge the Germans from their gun emplacements and bunkers, a sad consequence of war.

When we arrived at our first gun position, we were both physically and emotionally drained. So far we had seen only dead Germans and POWs. We fell into an exhausted sleep either on the ground or in the back of a truck. I slept in the back of the radio truck. We were awakened in the early morning of the following day by the battery sergeant major banging on an old galvanized bucket, not a pleasant sound especially as it seemed we had just fallen asleep. The battery water truck pulled up and we hurried to fill our two mess tins from one of the ten or so spigots. One tin held the day's drinking water. The other was divided into one half for our daily ablutions and the other half for dissolving our OXO-like cubes of tea, sugar and milk. It wasn't until two weeks later, when the major's bat man, a young British lad who, on the quiet, presented me with my own personal can of tea, that I had a decent cuppa – without milk or sugar. The food rations issued to the four batteries of the 59th

Regiment consisted of dehydrated foods, primarily oatmeal and a type of stew. We were also issued a soft, concentrated sort of wafer that we Newfoundlanders called biscuits, a couple of chocolate bars and eight blocks of the aforementioned concentrated tea, per day. This was our, so-called, basic battle rations.

Somewhere along the way, we received rations which carried the date 1916 as they had been packed for the British Army serving in Cairo, Egypt. They contained crackers and they were indeed crackers as you needed a sledgehammer to crack them. In fact, I once put one under the wheels of a moving truck and it remained intact. There was the option of soaking them for 24 hours or so which tended to soften them somewhat. If the bombs didn't kill us, we were at risk of death from antiquated provisions for sure. These 1916 rations contained other delectable items like powdered eggs, milk and potatoes.

I have heard from other sources that some other troops were much better fed than we were. If such was the case, perhaps they were a part of the elite group. For instance, Winston Churchill, in an address given on the BBC, said to the troops, "Men and women of the Army and Navy and gentlemen of the Air Force"… so obviously there was at least one superior group in the military and, as such, I suppose they merited superior food. In any case, our rations were what they were and, if we craved any luxury such as fresh fruit and vegetables, we yearned in vain. The quality of our food certainly improved once the Royal Army Service Corps (RASC) set up its depot in Rouen as it included a kitchen, and then we were able to indulge in such treats as freshly baked bread. Freshly baked homemade bread was long considered a staple in Newfoundland homes (and for me, even now; my wife's homemade bread is one of my most favourite things to eat). To be without bread, for long periods of time when we were on the move, was a real deprivation for many of us Newfoundlanders. I still remember how appreciative we were of our RASC bread when the kitchens were set up.

Our first task, at our new location, was to be the positioning of our batteries' four big 72 Gun Howitzers. However, Old "Lip" Witherick, our battery commander, insisted on morning inspection first. This was the same British Major Jim Witherick who was particularly disliked by practically every member of our battery. This was mostly because of his arrogance and disrespectful attitude toward us Newfoundlanders whom he considered to be stupid and quite inferior to himself. (In one of my interviews with Colonel Nicholson in regard to his book, *More Fighting Newfoundlanders*, his first question to me was, "Why did the major never attend any of the battery reunions?" And I told him the truth: it would have been detrimental to his well-being had he met up with any of his "underlings" in a civilian environment.)

A sorry sight we were in our work fatigues and, in spite of our best efforts, how much could we accomplish with a half mess can of water – probably a pint – with which to wash and shave? We had no access to even cold showers for at least another couple of weeks. By the time we received our first standard issues of two pairs of underwear, never the right size as they came in only two sizes, too big and too small, and two pairs of one-size fits all socks, we were far less than hygienic. Our dirty, stinky socks were sticking to our equally dirty, stinky feet, and our underwear was nothing to write home to your mother about.

Under the orders of Witherick, and against the advice of other officers, our first assignment was to dig a hole 30'x 30'x 6' for our gun emplacement. This was back-breaking work with pick and shovel and, after several hours of hard labour, we ran into solid rock and had to abandon the project. We then began a whole new strategy, probably engineered by some other officer(s) rather than Witherick, where we filled the metal containers that had held the cordite gun charges with the dirt from the ill-fated hole. We used these containers to erect a blast wall around the guns. We followed this much easier and more effective method of protecting our guns throughout the remainder of our stay in Normandy, and up through Belgium and Holland. Also, even though we had some natural concealment from the enemy in our first position, a number of gunners had engaged in further camouflaging the area thus providing us with some sense of added security.

It was at this first gun position that we were given a target, our first. We did not know what it was but, according to our orders, we fired all our guns in what we found out later was a success-ful attack on a concentration of German Tiger Tanks. What impact this had on any specific part of the war, I don't know, but we did destroy at least some of the enemy's weaponry.

Routine work continued until we packed up and began our move closer to Caen, the capital of the province of Normandy. We were unable to proceed all the way to Caen because the city was still being occupied by a powerful concentration of German troops and their heavy armour. They were most effectively blocking the route to Paris, still under the control of the pro-Nazi government, putting the enemy in a very strong strategic position.

Arriving at our destination, a few miles outside of Caen, we saw and heard a plane flying high over our heads. It made a couple of passes and then disappeared to the east with only its vapour trail remaining. I recalled a friend of mine, a RAF Flight Lieutenant, telling me about such a plane while we were in London at the Caribou Club. He said that such a strange sounding plane flying at such a high altitude could mean only one thing: it was a German reconnaissance plane (RECCE) equipped with a special diesel engine which accounted for its strange sound, and its mission was to photograph our position and our facilities. This intelligence was obviously relayed to the German Air Force who, consequently, dispatched bombers in an attempt to take out our position, and us. This was to be our first direct attack.

We had already set up our guns; the scammels (big trucks) had towed them into position and we now disconnected them as we moved back to the wagon line a few hundred yards behind the guns. Since we had taken over an area that had previously been occupied by the Germans, who had departed "plus vite," we discovered an adequate number of intact dugouts to accommodate the whole gun crew. However, a number of us separated from the gunners and dug our own slit trenches, each large enough for two. This was referred to as the buddy system. First we assembled a type of mattress by stuffing large bags with straw which we had scrounged from around the area. We called our creation "palliasses." We used four of our combined eight blankets to cover the palliasses and the remaining four became our top covers. Later, as we travelled throughout Europe, we improved our sleeping quarters by making use of the circular containers that the cordite charges had come in by flattening them and installing them on the inside of the trench. This brilliant innovation discouraged the moles from taking up residence in our luxurious quarters. We were relatively comfortable but slept fitfully never knowing what would happen at any given time. (Speaking of trenches reminds me of a story about a Newfoundland nurse who, in an attempt to escape a bombing incident, dove into a dugout. In relating the incident to a friend, she said, "Lucky thing I was able to dive into a wolfhole." "You mean a foxhole, don't you?" said her friend. To which she replied, "A fox might have dug it but a wolf was in it.")

At this particular time, before we got the opportunity to turn in for the night, a flare-bearing aircraft roared overhead, dropping its flares and illuminating our position as if it were daytime. The light allowed us and them to observe the assembled hundreds of allied tanks, guns and trucks, as far as the eye could see. The flares were followed in rapid succession by several German bombers. The first bombs fell on the tanks in an adjacent field destroying them and a number of the tanks' crews. In order to prepare for the night, tank crews had dug holes in the ground and then had driven the tanks over the top of the holes for protection. On this particular night, the bombers flew in over the hedge, about 2,000 or 3,000 feet over our heads, and directly hit a line of tanks killing the crews beneath them. And then it was our turn!

As they bombarded us, number four gun, under the command of Sergeant Dexter Rendell of Corner Brook, Newfoundland, took a direct hit and he was severely injured. Many of the gunners were hurt although none as seriously as was Lance Bombadier Rupert Bridger whose leg was blown off. A number of 200-pound shells, ammunition for our guns, were exploding and were being hit and detonated and, in the midst of all of this chaos, with flames shooting high into the air, cordite charges exploding and people frantically trying to protect and minister to Bridger, a voice from the higher echelons rang out, "Put out that torch!" as if a flashlight made any difference in that environment. An obliging gunner, with a well-directed blow to the command-giver, put out his "torch." We lost two of our members to shell shock and they were eventually returned to England as was wounded Lieutenant Art Dooling. (It is ironic that Art, who survived that horrible night, in later years died of a heart attack while shoveling snow in his driveway in St. John's.) As for myself, being basically a devout coward, all through this attack I felt that my life was about to end. However there was no safe haven and, even if there had been, I remembered that I was a soldier and I had a job to do. Like my fellow soldiers, I stiffened my backbone and "carried bravely on."

After dropping their load, the German bombers left the scene and headed back to their base of operations. The less serious injuries of many of the guns crews were attended to as well as they could be under the circumstances, and after Bridger had been evacuated to the nearest medical facility, we were able to assess our overall damage and to have a short period of rest and recovery. Incidentally, it has been recorded that our battery, the 22nd, was the hardest hit that night with eighteen 200-pound bombs falling in a quarter-acre space. The Roman Catholic Padre, viewing the area the next morning, commented that we Newfoundlanders must have had protection from on high to have survived the onslaught.

Caen was supposed to have fallen on D-Day but, since it was still being held by the German forces, a new strategy had to be formulated, and this was done under the command of British General Sir John Tredinnick Crocker. His proposal, which was instituted and carried out, involved the use of three infantry divisions, the Royal Navy's battleships including the HMS *Rodney*, with a powerful bombardment from their heavy guns, and 500 heavy bombers from the Royal Air Force with their 2,000-plus tons of high explosives. While sitting in my radio truck at the end of Carpiquet Airport runway, I personally witnessed the bombing raid carried out by the RAF, and what an awesome sight it was. After these combined powerful forces completed their mission, the 59th and other Heavy artillery units unleashed their devastating fire power to the tune of 600 guns. After the enemy had suffered massive destruction and loss, they had no option but to surrender, which they did, and the first Canadian Army entered Caen on the morning of July 9, 1944. There were still small pockets of resistance in and around the city, but these were effectively dealt with over a few days time.

After Caen had fallen, it was necessary to replenish our supply of shells, and so we made an ammunition run to the dump at St. Nicholas. For this operation, three-ton trucks and the strongest men in the battery were used. It took brute strength to load the 200-pound shells up onto the truck beds. The procedure was for the stronger man to take the heavier end of the shell on his shoulder while his partner lifted the higher end to his shoulder. Then the shell was maneuvered into position and rolled into the truck bed. Returning to the battery, unloading was a little easier because the shells were being rolled onto our shoulders from a higher level. However, this was still no simple task as each shell had to be carried to the appropriate site a short distance away. (Since most of us were barely out of our teens, it is no wonder many of us ended up with severe back problems which have plagued us throughout our lifetimes.)

On this trip, while returning to our battery, we were fired upon by two American P-47s. It was a good thing they were bad shots. There were no injuries to the crew and no damage was done to our shell-carrying trucks. All vehicles in the British Liberation Army were identified by the special markings of five point stars in circles. The bigger the vehicle, the bigger the marking was. Why the Americans fired on us, I have no idea. It could be they had poor eyesight, or perhaps the markings were not identifiable to them, or maybe they just needed some target practice!

Leaving Caen, we moved out onto the Monmouth Way, heading to our next gun position. The Monmouth Way had been bulldozed in a straight line stretching as far as the eye could see. Our regiment was lined up according to unit, each being separated from the next by about 20 feet. In peacetime, the normal spacing would have been much less, and using the peacetime spacing as the measuring agent, our assembled regiments with their massive amounts of equipment, guns, ammo and vehicles, would have stretched over a distance of 17 miles on the Monmouth Way.

As we moved along the Way, we saw many signs warning us of the German snipers who were, undoubtedly, hiding in cleverly camouflaged areas, awaiting our arrival. After several miles, we turned off the Monmouth Way onto a secondary road. We soon noticed three German graves that were not really graves but rather three individual areas, marked with three rifles, bayonettes attached, and stuck into the ground with German helmets atop each. There was no identification of any kind, a grim image of horrors of man's inhumanity to man.

We located our guns' positions, and the gun crews began their task of moving and setting up. This new area was too beautiful a setting for the action that would take place there. Rolling hills sloped into a gentle valley where our guns were assembled. There were shrubs and trees and an abundant variety of lovely wild flowers. "Peace on earth, goodwill towards man" seemed to be more appropriate to such a sight as this. Unfortunately, it was not to be.

As we were completing the set-up of the Lewis anti-aircraft machine gun, a German ME-109 came screaming in over the horizon, flying very low and strafing like crazy. He circled for a second pass and just as he passed directly behind us, he was hit by a British Bofors anti-aircraft gun. As he came over our position, he turned his plane upside down and bailed out. The plane crashed into a 25-pounder gun position ahead of us. The pilot's parachute opened and he came swinging down to the ground. An over-enthusiastic gunner, from our battery, began firing in his direction, which was, of course, against all regulations and moral ethics. He was immediately apprehended, as was the German pilot. I remember thinking that this German pilot certainly did not resemble what Hitler considered to be the perfect blond, blue-eyed Aryan. He looked more like he might have come from Spain or South America. In any event, he was one very scared individual and probably happy to become a POW rather then a casualty of war.

My job, during the course of battle, was that of a signalman and, as such, my position of operation was often in the gunpit. Lines ran between our four guns and the gun position officer. The officer would pass the pertinent information along to the individual guns for the appropriate action to be taken. In the late evening, after the incident with the German ME-109 and the German pilot's capture, I, not being involved with signals work at the time, was sent back by an officer to the wagon lines to get a flashlight. I retrieved it and started back in the direction of our gun site. As I passed the three German graves that we had seen earlier, a shot rang out...someone was trying to kill me! I was momentarily rooted to the spot but quickly recovered and started running towards a near-by cornfield and dove in. I very slowly and gingerly started crawling forward, not knowing whether or not I was still in the sniper's view or if he was perhaps in the cornfield with me, and when nothing happened, I forced myself to relax somewhat. It was by now nearly dark, so, as soon as I felt confident enough to leave the cornfield, I ran pell-mell back to the relative safety of our gun site. Since there had been only one shot, I began to think that maybe one of my "colleagues" had been trying to have a little fun at my expense, but no one looked guilty or said a word. I guess I was just one lucky soldier!

Shortly after this, and after we had completed our assignment at this site, we prepared to move out and head for the Falaise area. This was, as far as I can recall, the first week of August 1944. It was also the time when Hitler had decided to use the bulk of his remaining armour in a final desperate attempt to breach the British and Canadian lines running down the coast of France. The stand at Falaise was to counteract Hitler's plan to separate the British/Canadian forces from the Americans and weaken the Allies' position. This was Hitler's first try at getting access to the Belgian Seaport of Antwerp.

The Falaise Gap confrontation, between the Allied Forces and the 5th and 7th German Armies, was already in progress when we arrived. This battle proved to be one of the decisive, and most ferocious, of World War II. It resulted in more casualties than had been experienced during the first eleven months of the European engagement. Much of the Allies' success was due, in no small measure, to the heavy involvement of the Royal Air Force (RAF) fighter bombers and the United States 9th Air Force. The RAF Typhoon Fighters were most effective. These Fighters were armed with four rockets on each wing and they were being used for the first time in WWII. Others have suggested that Hitler had 1,000 bombers in reserve for engagement in such an encounter as this, but we saw no evidence that there was any resistance at all, from the air, by the Germans. The bombers and fighters zoomed in over the German troops at will, and at the end of the combat, the enemy was completely surrounded and had no option but to surrender, which they did en masse. While thousands of German POWs were being herded into cages, many thousands of Germans and Allied troops lay dead and strewn all over the area. What a human tragedy! A large number of the casualties and the prisoners appeared to be about our age. They were boys barely out of their teens, products of the Hitler Youth Movement, in many cases, fighting to defend their homeland. They believed they were championing a just cause and, like us, experienced the pain of separation from home, family and loved ones, and the possibility of never going home again. As we have discovered throughout history, war resolves nothing.

While the destruction from the air took place, the ground forces were mid-skirmish employing Armed Personnel Carriers (APC). These armoured vehicles were also being used for the first time, to rapidly move troops/infantry from place to place, where and when they were most urgently needed. Typically armed with only a machine gun, they were not designed for direct engagement but rather for safe transport, protected from ambush and shrapnel. From our vantage point, which had been set up some distance away while we were awaiting our orders to advance, we could recognize the various sounds of the weaponry being used in the ground combat. We could hear Schmeissers (German machine pistols), British Bren and Sten guns, tank guns and small machine fire, and the occasional pop of rifle fire from both sides. The unmistakable sounds of the ever-present ambulances, moving to and fro with wounded troops, both from the German and Allied camps, made us fully aware of the massive death and destruction occurring.

When we had first arrived at our site, it was imperative to prepare our slit trenches immediately after gun set-up. Even at this time, the famous and fearsome German 88s had been put into action. These guns were one of the most deadly weapons of the war. They were easily hidden in brush or in a fortified village. The multi-purpose weapons were being used to attack tanks, aircraft, ground crews and weaponry. They were very effective in counter-battery work and, since we were a battery and within their range, they were now ready to practice their expertise on us. We were forced to take refuge in our trenches on a number of occasions, and if anyone suggests they were not afraid during these times, I would have to respond that, in my opinion, they were lying. They were only mortal human beings like myself and I am not ashamed to use a Newfoundland expression and say, "I was scared s***less." As I lay in my cold and uncomfortable trench, the guns were firing constantly, and the shells were whistling and screaming overhead. I hoped they stayed up there and away from me.

All the same, I was now relatively calm. At the first close attack, I had been paralyzed with fear. After my initial shaking and shivering subsided somewhat, my body seemed to completely seize up and, as far as I can recall, I was unable to move even if there had been somewhere that I could have gone. Perhaps there was enough moisture in the trench to make my pants wet, but it certainly could have come from another source. The whole situation was so drastic and terrifying, and seemed to go on for so long, that I suspect even the groundhogs and moles were ready to seek the relative safety of our slit trenches. I remembered what an old-timer had said to me: "Don't worry Frank, you won't hear the shot that kills you." That was no consolation at all. It has been said that there are no atheists in foxholes, and I am inclined to agree. Since I grew up in the Salvation Army tradition, prayer was not an abstract to me, but I am sure that I was not the only one praying fervently when we found ourselves at death's door. It is strange though, how over time one can become desensitized to almost anything. Eventually, as these incidents continued to occur, we learned to tolerate them much better, undoubtedly tensing as an attack began but being able to loosen up to a certain extent, and almost to shrug it off as a common occurrence, believing and hoping that we would, as usual, survive. I must say the cordite blast walls of our trenches held up well and were certainly worth the effort we had put into erecting them. The Germans had not done this reinforcement job with their trenches and, consequently, they were more prone to death and injury from enemy fire than we were.

After the carnage of the Falaise Battle, the appropriate authorities from Britain, Canada and the United States dispatched their crews to recover and bury their dead. The POWs were sent to the Allied countries for processing. After this, we vacated our position and moved out to proceed to Cailly, a rest area.

Unless one has experienced the devastation of war firsthand, it is impossible to imagine the stench from the thousands of decaying bodies, not only of human bodies but also those of thousands of cattle, other animals and especially those of horses. The Germans had used horses to transport their guns and wagons and there were many carcasses strewn around the countryside, in the roadways and into prepared ditches. This whole scene was reminiscent of Dante's *Inferno* (a comparison I suggested to Colonel Nicholson in an interview for *More Fighting Newfoundlanders*; in his book he inadvertently attributed the comparison to Padre Farrell).

Sometime in late August of 1944, we arrived at Cailly, a small French village close to Louviers on the Ure River in central France. We felt entitled to and in need of this respite. We were billeted in a barracks that was said to have been the residence of a group of German Air Force personnel. It was a sturdy, well-constructed building and, I imagine, at the time of the former residents' occupancy, had been well-furnished and decorated. We found it practically empty and totally devoid of any finery. We slept on the floor on our palliasses and were happy to have a clean, dry place to lay our heads. It was far superior to any place we had been for quite some time. The farmers from the area around Eterville, a village close to Cailly, presented us with some of their locally grown vegetables and fruits, and in return we assisted them with their farm chores. It was with much gratitude that we accepted their gifts of French bread, sometimes hot from the oven, and on a few occasions, cheese and a bottle of wine as well. The French villagers were, for the most part, cordial, and were happy to entertain and socialize with us whenever they could. Our rest rejuvenated us and when we were ready to move on three or four weeks later, we felt more fit and capable of continuing on to our next position, to whatever mission awaited us there.

In 1977, the movie *A Bridge Too Far*, starring Robert Redford, Sean Connery, and Sir Laurence Olivier was released. This was based on an incident called Market Garden that occurred in the area where we were now positioned, and which took place about the time we moved there around the end of September 1944. We were not aware of it at the time, but the Germans had already overwhelmed an attempt by the Allies to establish a bridge across the Rhine River at Arnheim, as a route into Germany. It is widely believed, and the movie depicted this incident, that a member of the Dutch underground had tipped off the Germans and, as the Allied paratroopers bailed out of their planes, the German riflemen were ready and shot and killed them while they were still in the air. The surprise of the counter-attack, the tremendous strength of the enemy, and the terrible weather prevalent in the area at the time posed an insurmountable obstacle for the Allies, and they were forced to accept their defeat, deal with their losses, and to move forward to the next mission.

After the Market Garden defeat, the Allied troops moved toward the Leopold Canal in Belgium. This area, all around the entrance to the Scheldt Estuary, was rife with pockets of enemy resistance. For quite some period, from late October to late December of 1944, the 59th Regiment was being pressed into service when and where required, sometimes using the full complement of guns from the regiment and, at other times, single guns from different batteries, depending upon the specific need at the time. Weather conditions, to add to our woes, were beginning to deteriorate both in Belgium and in Holland. It was so cold that with the limited supply of winter clothing we had, which was not much more than gloves, we were ill-prepared to face the elements. Sometimes we discarded our inadequate leather boots, put on the three pairs of socks we each owned, and ran behind the trucks. This kept our feet from freezing and warmed up our bodies.

During this time we were billeted in our dugouts outside the small village of Eecloo, Belgium, close to the Leopold Canal, a pleasant area as yet untouched by the fighting. However, Antwerp, the rivers and canals around Antwerp, and most of the surrounding countryside were under German control. The waterways throughout the country had been intentionally flooded in an attempt to thwart the Allied advancement through Belgium and eventually on into Holland. Despite the cold, the ground was so wet that the eight-ton guns often moved from their mounted positions, sometimes turning over in the process of being fired. It required much effort and manpower to maneuver them back into position. However, we Newfound-landers, being great improvisers, devised alternative ways of solving the problem. In one instance, we used a scammel to move an unoccupied house off its concrete foundation, thus providing the ideal base for our gun platform.

As our occupancy of the Eecloo area continued, we found the time and opportunity to do some scrounging. We had learned from the locals that, up ahead, there were vegetable farms and fruit orchards. We figured we would try to supplement our diet by restocking our larders and dugouts with a fresh supply of whatever edible produce we could obtain. It was during one such expedition that a few fellows from our battery decided to go a little too far afield, not realizing that perhaps the Germans had moved closer to our unit. We had heard gunfire and seen tracers during the night. The guys had used poor judgment and as a result found themselves under German fire on the banks of the canal. Gunner Paddy Brennan had even strayed down over the canal's bank where, unfortunately for him, a German sniper shot and hit him dead on. Bleeding profusely, he fell forward half-in and half-out of the water. While this was going on, a sergeant from the Lincoln and Welland Infantry, a Canadian Regiment, was preparing to launch an attack across the canal. To attempt to rescue Paddy, he would be jeopardizing his mission by exposing his position to the enemy. Nevertheless, he offered to provide fire coverage if Paddy's friends would try and save him. This they did and, despite the continuous gunfire from the sniper, they pulled Paddy up over the embankment and to an area where an ambulance was waiting to evacuate him to the nearest military hospital, the 12th Canadian General Hospital in Bruges, Belgium. Paddy seemed to be seriously injured, so much so that he was bleeding from the mouth and we were holding out little hope for his survival. I heard that Paddy had eight German bullets in him. (Big surprise! While serving as a member of the RCAF in Goose Bay, Labrador, in 1956, I was visiting a civilian club there when I heard a distinct voice which sounded exactly like Paddy: "Old Tannoy," the name of a British loudspeaker, was our nickname for him. Sure enough, there was Paddy Brennan, hale and hearty and working as a pipe-fitter for the Canadian Army in Goose Bay. I do not know if he had been as badly injured as we surmised or if he was just one extra tough Newfoundlander. He nearly died of shock when he saw me and vice versa.)

Since the Allies had failed to establish the Bridge at Arnheim and we had completed our mission in the Leopold Canal region in Belgium, our regiment received orders to move forward to another area where other batteries were already actively engaging the enemy. Many squirmishes and several major battles were waged before we eventually reached Venlo in Holland on the border of Holland and Germany.

In Venlo, we were fortunate to be offered the use of a henhouse. It was on the property of a Dutch farmer who, with his wife and two or three children, lived in the farmhouse nearby. The weather had turned quite cold so we were looking forward to being billeted in a relatively warm and dry building for a change. After evicting the hens from their abode, we had a little difficulty in persuading King Rooster to vacate. He was not happy about being separated from his harem and wanted the hens back in rather than him having to follow them out. Once we successfully evacuated the hens from the henhouse, we set about the task of making it livable, the most daunting task being to get rid of the henhouse smell. A wide open door, with the brisk Dutch breezes blowing through, did much to alleviate the situation. We stuffed our palliasses with straw and, with whatever useable material we could find, constructed a stove of sorts. In Newfoundland, for as many years as I can remember, a Home Comfort range was a popular heater and cook stove. Although our improvisation did serve the purpose of heating and cooking, it was by no stretch of the imagination a Home Comfort! But as long as we were not expecting any miracles, like a lot of heat or well-cooked food, our makeshift cooking heater did the job.

Our Christmas rations we decided to present to the farmer's wife. She very graciously accepted our offering and promised to combine it with whatever she could contribute from her larder, and to make us, and her family, the best Christmas dinner possible. I don't remember exactly what our Christmas rations were but they were an improvement over our regular issue, for sure. The children were delighted with the chocolate bars and candy we gave them, and the farmer more than appreciated his gift of cigarettes, especially since he had an extra number from those of us who did not smoke. I don't remember giving the farmer's wife anything so I hope she shared the children's candy. She certainly outdid herself in the food she prepared and even mustered up what decorations she could to make our "new digs" look festive.

All too soon, just as we were beginning to feel comfortable with our newfound family and our renovated henhouse, we received our orders to move from Venlo southwards toward Ardennes where there was a large build-up of German troops, tanks, artillery and infantry, on the Siegfried Line. The Siegfried Line was a line of defence stretching from the North Sea all the way down to Spain. This line was supposed to be impenetrable, but the same supposition had been made concerning the Maginot Line in France, and the Germans had solved that problem by going around and over it. In an effort to prevent them from another such action, American General Dwight Eisenhower requested help from the British General Bernard Montgomery. Montgomery responded to the request by dispatching, from their position north of Venlo, the 30 Corps, and they joined us while we were en route to Malmedy, Belgium.

Before we reached Malmedy, and because darkness would soon overtake us, we decided to overnight in a farmer's field. We were not in the habit of travelling at night and did so only on the rare occasion when we had no other option. In such a case, we had very limited lighting as the vehicles headlights were not much larger than a quarter. The trucks' differentials were painted white and a small white bulb provided the only illumination in that area. The gun, which was being towed backwards, had a small red light on the end of the muzzle, and the driver of the vehicle following used that light as his guide. There was one incident when the tiny red light on the gun ceased to function and the vehicle behind kept on moving, right into the gun, which broke through the windshield and pinned the driver's arm to the truck cab's wall. It was dangerous enough travelling in the daytime; we didn't need the extra stress of travelling in the darkness. We set up for the night and, while my partner took the first watch on the truck's radio, I went to sleep in my makeshift bed in the farmer's barn. It seemed like only a very short time when I was awakened by the sound of machine gunfire, and it sounded very close. I rolled out of bed as I was trained to do and, when the gun noises stopped, ventured outside to investigate. I was told that a number of soldiers wearing American uniforms and speaking perfect American English had just been killed or captured. Actually, they were Germans disguised as Americans, attempting to infiltrate and disrupt our operations. It was learned, from one of the prisoners, that they belonged to a commando troop, under the orders of Hitler's most daring commando, Colonel Otto "Scarface" Skorzeny – dubbed by the Allies as the most dangerous man in Europe. This was a part of the same group which had engaged in all sorts of espionage activities since we first landed on the beaches in Normandy. They were setting up boobie traps wherever they were likely to cause the most damage, poisoning wells and orchards, etc. This particular unit had drawn attention to themselves when Allied Intelligence discovered that road signs along the routes most used by the Allied troops were being reversed in an effort to confuse the drivers. Luckily for us, these individuals were being tracked and, consequently, apprehended before they could execute their diabolical plans.

After the commandos had been dealt with, we began our move southward toward Malmedy and Bastogne in the Ardennes. The Battle of the Bulge was unfolding. News concerning the activity of the Germans in the area was very slowly seeping through to us, and we learned that the enemy's drive towards Antwerp was gathering steam. The Americans were putting up a brave fight but they were badly outnumbered, by about ten to one, by the Germans, and were desperately in need of assistance. In the meantime, our progress toward Malmedy to come to their aid was not going well. The roads were covered with ice, and blowing snow was restricting our vision. The job of handling the load of some 20 tons was a difficult one. The scammel was towing the gun, which weighed eight tons, a gun crew of eight men, plus eight 200-pound shells and other ammunition and weaponry. The gun was attached with an extra heavy trailer hitch and was being pulled by the scammel. Taking into consideration the convoy connection set-up, the deplorable conditions of the roads, and the weather, the possibility of a mishap was ever present. We moved as fast as we could but, all the while, the conditions for the Americans at Bastogne were gradually deteriorating and we were only too well aware of that.

Usually, when we were on a lengthy move, our mobile kitchen would leave ahead of us and, after a few hours on the road, they would find a convenient spot, set up and have tea and sandwiches ready for us when we arrived. Before reaching

Malmedy, the kitchen had been set up near a Belgian farm-house and, because it was so stormy and cold, our NCO (non-commissioned officer) requested permission from the farmer for us to go into his house to eat our lunch and to warm up. The farmer was understandably rather reluctant. He had already had dealings with the Germans a few days earlier and he was not sure he should trust us. In my best high school French – "*Nous sommes amis*" – I tried to persuade him that we were okay and he finally relented and admitted us. He was not confident enough, however, to allow his children to accept the gifts of chocolate and candy we offered. One of our guys, exasperated by the reception we were getting, pulled out his bayonette and stuck it on his rifle…that did a lot to prove how wonderful we were! Of course, he had no intention of causing any harm. Since we were not in the habit of intimidating innocent people, our sergeant made him put the bayonette back into its sheath. The treats were left on the table and after some friendly chitchat between us all, the farmer realized we meant no harm and allowed his children to indulge. By the time we were ready to leave and resume our journey to Malmedy, everyone was smiling.

Before we reached the area where the Battle of the Bulge was being fought, and General George Patton and his army had arrived from the south of France, and because the United States Air Force had been unable to engage in the battle due to weather conditions, the Germans were confident of their ultimate victory over the Americans. In fact, the German commanding officer sent three of his officers to American General Anthony McAuliffe, bearing a white flag of truce and a written surrender demand.

The General's reply to the surrender ultimatum was given in one word, "NUTS!" The German Commander was puzzled and he asked, "*Vas ist das* NUTS?" to which McAuliffe replied, "It means drop dead!" and he tore up the surrender demand paper and threw it into the wind. The outnumbered Americans continued to persevere until finally, to their great relief, assistance arrived by way of the American 3rd Army under Patton, and 30 Corps British Army, of which our 59th Newfoundland Artillery Regiment from Holland was a part. The situation rapidly improved but we were still in need of more powerful aid if things were going to turn around in the Allies' favour. Well, we did get what many considered to be an act of divine intervention. Miraculously, it seemed, the sky cleared, and as it opened up, a myriad of planes appeared overhead. American B17s and Liberators, and the British RAF's Lancasters came roaring in, dropping their bombloads as they flew overhead. They were too numerous to count, hundreds, perhaps thousands of planes. The ground forces intensified their battle. Under the tremendous assault of our gun Howitzers, firing their 200-pound shells, and the resulting killing power of the airbursts combined with the relentless pounding of Patton's Third Army, the confidence which the Germans had so arrogantly displayed was quickly dissipating and they were in absolute disarray. The rapidity and ferocity with which the Allies attacked had completely overwhelmed them and consequently resulted in their surrender. With the miracle of the ground forces arriving almost simultaneously, just at the right time, and the sky clearing, right on cue, Bastogne, which had been so badly off that it had been on the verge of surrender, was given new life and the ability to continue fighting. The Battle of the Bulge was finally over!

So many dreadful things had been happening in that area before we arrived that it's no wonder everyone gave a great sigh of relief when the Allies finally prevailed. We learned of some of the terrible atrocities that had been inflicted on the American Troops by the Germans, such as the Malmedy Massacre. On December 17, 1944, just before our arrival in Bastogne, the Germans, under SS Standartenführer Joachim Peiper, had defeated and captured about 120 American troops, corralled them in a field, and then fired on them with machine guns.

The Americans, however, engaged in a little retaliation. According to a story they told, while General Patton's Army stopped on a hill above the Bulge, before entering the battle, they observed a crew of Germans in the act of stealing gas from the American refueling point. The Americans removed a few 45-gallon drums of gas from one of their trucks, took off the tops and inserted short fuses. They put the drums in position at the top of the hill, set them on fire and started them in motion. Some exploded on the way down while the other flaming fireballs rolled into the midst of the Germans.

It is said that all is fair in love and war but sometimes "all" goes a little too far, I think. In any event, the Battle of the Bulge was over and it was time for use to vacate the area and leave the mop-up operations to others. The 59th Newfoundland Regiment had done its part and had served honourably.

While we were awaiting our new orders, our regiment engaged in the required maintenance of vehicles and guns. This was a slow process as the frigid weather hindered our efforts. It was also a factor in determining when we would move back to Holland to rejoin the British troops who remained engaged in battle there. There were still pockets of German resistance in the area north of Venlo, closest to Arnheim, where the Allies were attempting to secure a bridge over the Rhine River to gain access into Germany. In the meantime, an old sinus ailment of mine had flared up and, since the medical officer had done all he could to treat it, it was decided to evacuate me out to the hospital in Bruges. The ambulance that transported me to the hospital had two other patients, one an American stretcher patient named Harvey Waters, and the other a young German member of the fanatic Hitler Youth, who appeared to be about 16. They were both being dropped off at an American medical post, the young German because he was an American prisoner of war.

Harvey was in very poor shape. He told me he had been trapped, for several days, in a hole in the floor of a house that was being occupied by Germans. He had become so dehydrated that he had resorted to urinating on his hands to moisten his lips. He could hardly believe he had survived the ordeal and was still alive, even if only barely. (Several times over the years, I tried to contact Harvey at his New Jersey, US, address. When I was unsuccessful, I assumed he had died from his wounds. However, a couple of years ago my daughter, who lives in the US, googled the Railsplitters Division of the Airborne Unit of which Harvey had been a part and discovered three Harvey Waters in the New Jersey area. The three might have been WWII veteran Harvey, his son, and grandson. If Harvey were still alive he would have been about 90, a ripe old age after under-going the injuries of war.)

As for the young German prisoner, when I was about to enter the ambulance, a military policeman had given me a revolver with the comment, "That little bastard could be dangerous.

Protect yourself if necessary." I noticed the poor soul was having trouble keeping his pants up, and he was obviously suffering the ill effects of some form of malnutrition. He was wild-eyed and spewing forth a barrage of obscenities, praise for his Führer, curses on his enemy, etc. I could not understand much of what he was saying but it was hard not to feel empathy toward him. Here he was so young, indoctrinated into the Nazi philosophy since he was a child, believing he was fighting for a just cause, taught to hate and, undoubtedly, frightened to death. However, it was my job to be vigilant and to protect, not only myself, but the helpless Harvey. The best I could do, since he was having trouble keeping his pants on, was to relieve him of his belt. Then he would have to hold them up. With only one free hand, he would have difficulty in tackling me as I was young, strong and relatively fit. And because we were nearing the end of the conflict, and he would not be involved in any further fighting, he might be fortunate enough to have been rehabilitated into a new and better life. (After all these years, I still have that belt, and I have often thought how wonderful it would be if I could contact him and return his belt and find that he was living a happy healthy life. He was, after all, a boy like me, caught in something way bigger than ourselves.)

When I arrived at the hospital in Bruges, I was processed and admitted for treatment. It was a huge facility with a special ward for wounded prisoners of war, under constant guard, who were being treated before being transferred to POW camps for internment. In the course of time, I struck up a conversation with a mild-looking German prisoner. He spoke English very well, and he talked about his family and also of the Bulge. He described the devastating fire power exerted by the Allies, of which the 59th Regiment was a large part, and the tremendous casualties the Germans had suffered as a result. It was at times like this that I realized how much both sides had suffered. Our big guns, the 72 Howitzers and our 200-pound shells, had saved our lives but had destroyed thousands of other human beings. Many of our enemy had not wanted war any more than we did. They had families, had the desire to live peaceful lives, and felt no more animosity towards us than we did towards them. They were fighting to satisfy the whims of a maniacal leader. Many soldiers had been forced to fight with the Third Reich as the Germans overran the countries of Poland, Hungary, France, Holland, Czechoslovakia, Austria, Norway, Denmark, Belgium, Luxembourg and others. The wounded German broke down in tears and, with everything else he had to endure, he admitted to being hungry. The meal trays had passed him by, intentionally he thought, on several occasions. I mentioned this to the orderly and the German did get a meal at that time, but it only confirms the fact that prisoners, even wounded prisoners, were not always treated with kindness on either side of the fence.

After I had undergone treatment and surgery at the 12th Canadian General Hospital in Bruges, it was decided to air evacuate me back to England. The cold damp weather of France, Belgium and Holland had played havoc with my sinus condition and it had affected my entire body. I was flown from Bruges to Swindon, an RAF base in Wiltshire, and from there by ambulance to the hospital in Nottingham. Alex Hewitt, who had served in the 59th Regiment, had also been returned to England for similar reasons, as had Eric Rowsell, from Corner Brook, who had served with the 166th Regiment in Italy. After our various treatments and our recuperation periods were over, we were returned to the Depot at Norwich. We worked for the next few weeks in the communication center there. During the first week of May 1945, we were given a three day pass to London where we stayed at the Newfoundland Caribou Club. On May 8, I was on Trafalgar Square when the news we had been awaiting came – "The War is Over – Victory in Europe is a Reality!" Bedlam followed. People went crazy, shouting, singing, dancing, crying, kissing everyone in sight, and it is said that everyone in London between the ages of nine and 90 got drunk, a slight exaggeration I think, but it was the best of times! As usual, some people got a little too elated and did stupid things like climbing atop lampposts. In one incident, a British sailor climbed a lamp pole and, while wildly swinging his arms, lost his balance and fell to the sidewalk below. He didn't move and the ambulance came and took him away. I do not know whether or not he died, but if not, he was certainly badly injured. It was both ironic and sad that he had survived the rigours of war only to die or to sustain serious harm on VE Day in London.

After much celebration in the streets and at other places including the Caribou Club, we returned to the Norwich Depot to await our notice of embarkation back to Newfoundland. Finally, we boarded the troop ship and headed out. I remember very little of what occurred in England between the time VE Day was declared and the time we left England to return to Newfoundland, and about the crossing. I suppose it was because my mind was saturated with all we had experienced since leaving Newfoundland in 1942, and it would take some time to process it all and to be able to return to some semblance of normal living.

I do know that our return voyage was much more uneventful, tranquil and safe than had been our Atlantic passage to England. We tied up at Harvey's Dock; the same dock from which we had departed St. John's and which was still enshrouded in fog. We were home! Everything seemed the same, but everything was not the same for those of us who had gone to war. How would it ever be again? Like many others, I left home when I was 18, carefree, naive and inexperienced, and returned at 23, having seen more in those few years than I ever expected in a lifetime. Of course, we were grateful to have played a part in the defeat of Hitler. Yet who could possibly forget the enormous cost of victory? Millions had died in the conflict, millions of wounded would suffer the remainder of their lives, and six million Jews had been exterminated in the gas chambers of camps throughout Europe. Children would grow up without fathers. Countries had been completely destroyed. The horrors of war were firmly imprinted on our minds and could never be forgotten.

When we disembarked in St. John's, we were transported in the bed of a large truck to Shamrock Field for our welcome home celebration. We were stopped momentarily near a beer supply truck when one of our number reached over and helped himself to a case, a reward, he said, for all the hard work we had done. At Shamrock Field, we listened to the customary speeches and were given tickets to our hometowns. As we were dismissed, I am sure we all wondered how we would adjust to our civilian lives and where we would go from here. As for me, I would, first of all, walk to Duckworth Street to visit my Uncle Nathan and to retrieve my pants with the one pressed leg if Aunt Louie hadn't already disposed of them.

My transportation from St. John's to Corner Brook was by way of the beloved Newfie Bullet, the train that went across Newfoundland from St. John's to Port-aux-Basques, a distance of about 560 miles in about 30 hours, a veritable bullet indeed!

To my great delight, it was taking me home. After the joyful reunion with family and friends, it was time to relax and spend some time trying to formulate a plan for moving on with my life. In October 1945, with other soldiers, I returned to St. John's for formal discharge. From there, I had decided to go to Saint John, New Brunswick, to attend the Radio College of Canada.

PART TWO

My first job after Radio College was at the receiver site in Gander, Newfoundland.

In the early 1940s, before the advent of jets, Gander International Airport, because of its strategic location, was a beehive of activity. All aircraft crossing the Atlantic were required to land there for refueling. During WWII, and before my time there, Gander International Airport was of considerable importance because it was the base for Ferry Command. Ferry Command were pilots, both male and female, who flew fighter aircraft from the United States and Canada, through Gander, to the United Kingdom and then Europe for dispersal to strategic locations to engage in combat missions. After this and into the 1960s radio communications was an integral part of the Gander airport's operations.

As a member of the radio operators' ground crew my job was to maintain constant contact with the flying aircraft and to pass pertinent information, including current weather conditions, to my airborne counterparts. Our radio site was set apart from the main International Passenger Terminal, so we did not often see the international business types, politicians and government officials and movie stars passing through. At first, it was quite a spectacle to observe celebrities milling around the terminal, or sitting around at the Big Dipper Bar Lounge refreshing themselves, but in time, the lustre faded and sightings became quite commonplace so that many of the airport staff, including the janitorial and security personnel, were no longer overly impressed by most of the travellers – though Nikita Krushchev and Marilyn Monroe may have proved exceptions.

My job as radio operator in Gander was interesting enough to hold my attention for awhile. I had been introduced to Morse code during my Boy Scout days, and, after my radio college education, I was happy to have the opportunity to use my skills in the sending and receiving of Morse code traffic. However, social life in Gander was practically non-existent, and as a junior operator my advancement opportunities were limited, so I soon decided it was time to move on to greener fields, and possibly to a little adventure. So, I went to Toronto.

On arriving, an old family friend was able to find living accommodations for me with a Newfoundland family. I had no idea how long it would take me to find a job in the communications field, but I did know I needed to find some kind of work to supplement my rather meager savings. While scanning the Toronto newspapers, I saw an ad, from a nearby business, seeking the services of persons to pour lead pots for use in the construction industry. It sounded simple enough, and it was, but I was not good at it...my loud Hungarian boss agreed with me.

After a few days of his shouting at me in his native language, none of which I understood except for his frequent use of referring to me as a *"Dummkopf"* – I knew this label was not complimentary – I threw my ladle of molten lead back in the cauldron, evacuated the work site, and became a member of the unemployed again. My next job was with Hydro Electric Power Company (HEPC), as an office assistant...boring, and not at all suited to my personality, so I was soon on the move again, wandering around like a man without a country, and without purpose. Then, another opportunity presented itself, one that would get me outside to work and, at the same time, provide me with a great view of the city of Toronto: a job as a slater's helper working the Queen's Park Ontario Government Building, approximately 100 feet high, replacing the slates and copper draining system. At this time, in the 1950s, safety precautions were not as they are today, so this job proved to be a rather dangerous one. Looking back, I believe I must have been employed by a scab company. There was no professional scaffolding to reach the slating area so we rigged our own and took our chances; there were no safety harnesses or safety nets so it was a matter of being extremely careful and extremely lucky. Thank God that before any mishap befell me, I learned about a United Nations team that had come from New York to the city of Toronto on a recruitment mission; they were looking for communication personnel skilled in Morse code. I was offered a position, and left my dangerous job to go to work with the United Nations in New York and, eventually ended up in Korea. A safer spot than the roof of the Legislative Buildings of Toronto?...I think not!

The Korean War (1950–53) was a major Cold War Military clash fought up and down the peninsula of Korea. The Communist states of the Democratic People's Republic of Korea (North Korea), China and the Soviet Union were arrayed against the Republic of Korea (South Korea), supported by the United States and a multi-nation United Nations force. It ended in a stalemate in 1953 that restored the boundaries to nearly what they were at the start, along the 38th parallel.

The Korean War was already in progress when I arrived, and the fighting had proceeded as far as the Yalu River, the dividing line between China and North Korea. The Americans, Canadians, Australians, New Zealanders and a few others, were involved in the conflict. As far as the Canadian government was concerned, this was not a war, but merely a United Nations' police action, which did not in any way negate the fierce combat that was going on there. Under the United Nations, many Military Observers, including those from Holland, Pakistan, Thailand, El Salvador and other countries, were keeping a wary eye on the situation as events unfolded. Again, as had happened in the European wars, bad weather was a significant factor in the outcome of troop performance. The continental climate in that part of the world, with the wild winds blowing in from Russia, Mongolia, and from all over that frigid area, played havoc with personnel and with the equipment of war.

The North Koreans attacked while shouting, screaming, blowing horns and beating drums. This style of fighting was frightening and appeared to us to be wild and out of control. It was in stark contrast to the precision of Hitler's Army in World War II. The frenzied intensity of the North Korean's seemingly chaotic style of warfare caught us off guard. All wars are brutal, as was certainly the case in World Wars I and II, but the conflict in Korea was in a class all by itself.

At that time, there was said to be about 35,000 North Korean and Chinese fighters south of the 38th parallel that was the dividing lone between North and South Korea. They made forays into Seoul on a regular basis, looking for battle and also for any food, clothing or money they might be able to steal.

One day, Colonel White, of the Canadian Army, and I went on a fact-finding mission to Pyongyang, the North Korean capital. We started out in our military jeep, and perhaps because the inhabitants did not recognize the United Nations insignia, they began throwing bricks at us. We were forced to return to Seoul without completing our mission. We, a group of Military Observers, were billeted in the Korean Military Advisory Group Compound (KMAGC) in Sobbingo, not far from Yong Dong Po Airport. There, because the enemy was famous for their ability to infiltrate the compound, to break windows, and to toss grenades into the buildings, heavy mesh wire was installed on all the windows. They countered this by bringing shears with them and cutting the wire. Consequently, we were issued American Army weapons, 45 automatics and carbines and, at night, we would hang them on our gunbelts on the bedposts so as to have them always near at hand. The enemy was so adept at avoiding surveillance and at being able to gain entrance to the compound that our method of defence was probably not a wise one. However, we were fortunate enough to avoid being shot or directly engaged. We were supposedly being guarded by the Republic of Korea (ROK) sentries, outside the compound, but they were not very effective and didn't instill any degree of confidence in us as they often ran away and hid when attacked. There was a recreation centre in the compound. On one occasion, while we were watching a movie, infiltrators came in on the roof and managed to toss a couple of grenades inside before they could be apprehended. The building was damaged and three or four people were either killed or injured. Even though we were only the short distance of approximately a half mile from our accommodations, we never walked anywhere at night in the compound, always using jeeps or ambulances for transportation. In another incident, a woman entered the compound to post notices on the bulletin board, or so she said. Someone accidentally jostled her, dislodging a cache of grenades which she was carrying on her head!

Before long we were moved and billeted in the Chosun Hotel in Seoul, which was decidedly a safer location for us. Things proceeded normally for the next few weeks until a plan was formulated to evacuate the military observers, including our group, to an area where the fighting was less concentrated. We were to be sent to Pusan (now Busan) at the southernmost tip of the Korean Peninsula.

Before this could happen, I was dispatched to Haneda, an airport near Tokyo, to assist with work as a radio operator. One night in Tokyo, while returning from the Yashimo Hotel to the Marunouchi Hotel, which had been taken over by the Armed Forces of New Zealand, I got lost. Tokyo is divided into districts and I knew if I could find out what district I was in I would be able to make my way back to the hotel. I stopped two Japanese men on the street and asked them where the Marunouchi Hotel was. They spit in my face and began to close in on me, shouting. More seemed to join them. I was terrified. I suddenly recalled the notice that I had read in the American Club on the Ginza, that the streets were increasingly dangerous and that Americans had recently been killed. Fortunately for me, an American Military Police jeep came along right at the moment and the Japanese dispersed. As far as I was concerned, had they not come by, I could have been killed. To this day, I still shudder every time I think about it.

When I finally returned to Korea, I learned that the formation plan to go to Pusan had not come to fruition and a considera- tion was being made to send me to Bangkok, Thailand. This plan also fell through as the military deposed King Rama IX in the "Radio Coup," during which a United Nations Military Observer had been killed. Meanwhile, while the UN Observers seemed to be in some degree of disarray, even more Chinese, millions of them, were pouring over the North Korean border, down into South Korea and converging on the United Nations troops. The fighting was so fierce that the UN troops were on the verge of collapse. North Korea and its allies, meanwhile, were alarmed at the high rate of casualties among the Chinese soldiers, and facing great obstacles supplying their front lines. The fighting entered a protracted stalemate, followed by a shaky truce. The parties concerned met at the 38th parallel which was to become, and still is, the demarcation line dividing North and South Korea. There, the Peace Treaty was signed at Panmunjom. Shortly after this, I returned to New York. Feeling that I had finally had my fill of the craziness associated with war, I decided to return to my roots in Corner Brook.

But before I was able to obtain suitable and permanent employment there, an interesting opportunity presented itself. I was approached by Albert Park, a retired Royal Air Force Officer, about participating in a census-taking, the first since Newfoundland had joined Confederation in 1949. It would involve four people, namely a boat captain, a cook named Albert, a chap from Western Newfoundland, and myself. We were to cover the Northern Peninsula from Martin's Point in Bonne Bay to Big Brook in the vicinity of Cape Bauld. I was somewhat acquainted with this area because I had taken my first sea voyage there when I travelled this northern route from Frenchman's Cove en route to St. John's to enlist in 1940. We would be travelling in a 30-foot boat over a distance of approximately 200 miles, 'as the crow flies.' Actually, considering that we visited all the little communities along the coast, we covered many additional miles. Port Saunders, Flower's Cove, Port aux Choix and Daniel's Harbour were the largest of the dozen or so communities along the coast. Other settlements were quite remote, in out-of-the-way places, without electricity and other services, and without roads to connect them to the larger centres. At first we felt that the locals were regarding us with some suspicion. Confederation had made us New Canadians and with that there was a proliferation of outsiders, all along the coast, doing business and asking all sorts of questions. So the many strangers milling around were sometimes suspect. When we reminded the people of the benefits they would be deriving from the new government such as Old Age Pension, Unemployment Benefits etc., and that we were there to list all the names so that no one would be left out, that changed the water on the beans! Joey Smallwood, in the course of campaigning for Confederation, was the harbinger of all things he considered "good" for the people of Newfoundland. Of course, he made promises galore, one of the most appealing being the payment of a Children's Allowance since people had very large families and could certainly use the extra money. The pension was to prove another powerful enticement for many people who had most likely never before seen a ten dollar bill in their lives. Smallwood had preached on these two topics for the duration of his many trips around the province. He became so endeared to his "subjects" that his portrait often replaced those of Jesus, the Virgin Mary and the Pope in their kitchens, dining rooms or bedrooms.

Speaking of large families, many had 10 to 12 children, and others as much as 17 to 20. In some small communities, there were only one or two family surnames, which suggested some cases of inter-family marriage. I remember in one household of many kids, I asked the mother why one of the children had a different surname than the others, to which she replied, "I had she before I married he," pointing to her husband. In one large family, the father had to get out the Bible because he couldn't remember the chronological order of his children's births and he had trouble with their names. It seems that after the common names, like Ruth, Esther, Peter and Joshua were used up, the difficult Bible names like Jeremiah, Hosea and others were called into action. We ourselves needed the Bible to get some of the spellings correct!

Generally speaking, the 32-day trip was engaging and most people were happy to interact with us. Food-wise, we ate a lot of fish, most of it caught right off the stern of our boat. We also ate mounds of homemade bread and bologna. We bought berries such as bakeapples, raspberries and blueberries when they were available from the locals. If one wanted an alcoholic drink, it was not available as I believe they thought we might also be government men who might make trouble for them. Thus it was a long and tiresome trip back to Corner Brook but, for the most part, our census-taking excursion was a pleasant enough experience and we had met some real nice Newfoundlanders... Whoops! Nice Canadians.

In Corner Brook I worked at the pulp lab at Bowater's Pulp and Paper Mill, where I stayed for about two years. During that time, in 1953, I married Ruby Moores. I also formed a dance band and, although I enjoyed the gigs at which we played at least once a week, I wasn't particularly enamored with my day job, so what do I do? I re-enlisted in the military, of course, going into the Royal Canadian Air Force (RCAF) as a communications person.

Because of my experience in both WWII and in Korea, and my Radio College education, I did not need further training at this time and so quickly received my first posting to Goose Bay, Labrador. There were no battles there except with the snow, 225 inches of it that first winter. Even with such abundance, some radar people working up on the Pine Tree Line were running short of water to make coffee. Everyone who was capable of swinging a shovel, even the base commanding officer, worked around the clock to keep the snow off the flat-roofed buildings to prevent their collapse.

We lived on Spruce Street, a main street in Goose Bay, in what was called a "steel locks." These were flat-roofed one-storey buildings joined together as duplexes. They were comfortable and well-furnished. Air Force buses provided free transportation around the base, to the Department of Transport and to the American side where approximately 10,000 American personnel, mostly US Air Force, were based. I remember getting off at the bus stop, just in front of our residence, and being unable to see the house. There was so much snow that steps were dug up to the top of the banks over which we walked and, by gradual steps, down over the bank into our dwelling. We survived that first winter and got through the second with a normal amount of snowfall. Then at the end of the second year we were transferred to Ontario. By this time, we were a little sorry to leave Goose Bay! We had enjoyed the weather there, in spite of all the snow of our first winter and the swarms of black flies that plagued us in the summer. There was no shortage of recreational activities in Goose Bay including hockey, curling, dances, etc. We were able to shop at the American PX for food and for specialty items like clothing, jewellery and other things, all of exceptional quality and of great value. Besides we were getting a Northern allowance and, because Goose Bay was a rather isolated place in the mid-1950s, we were granted extra leave and we were able to take a ten-day vacation in Montreal. Other members of the military were eager to go to Goose Bay for the same reasons that we were loath to leave there after our two-year posting. I must also add that there was always considerable activity going on at the American base due to the conflict between Europe and the Middle East at the time. There was a constant flow of American fighter planes and bombers flying in and out. There was also enough "transport" between Goose Bay and Harmon Field in Stephenville that we were frequently able to take advantage of the Americans' generous offer of a ride so that we could visit our families in Corner Brook.

We settled in Trenton, Ontario, where we loved the area with its boating and camping facilities, and beautiful farmlands with their great supply of the fresh fruits and vegetables which had definitely been in short supply in Goose Bay. My wife, Ruby, found a teaching job she loved. Then one day as I was typing up some traffic, I wrote, "CF [Chesley Frank] Dyke transferred to Fort Churchill, Manitoba, effective October 5th, 1959." So soon? (My Newfoundland reaction? I was some mad!) However, off we went, rage and all.

It was cold, desolate and depressing, with the winds blowing in off of Hudson Bay enough to freeze the arse off you. We eventually moved into the downtown area, as we didn't have the necessary number of points to warrant one of the limited numbers of married quarters on the base. That meant I had to travel back and forth to work, past the naval headquarters which was midway between the town site and the base. Sometimes I rode in the military truck and sometimes in the back of the military truck, so I could direct the driver with a few bangs on the cab when he couldn't keep his windshield clear enough from the snow and wind to be able to see the road. We usually spotted a polar bear or two en route. They used to come up to forage through the garbage cans from the hospital and the base kitchens. There was always lots of food available to them so they never had to resort to eating humans. The polar bears came to be so plentiful and such a nuisance that the RCMP and Provost Corps began scaring them off with flares and thunder flashes. I remember one night, Nicky, a telephone operator and a friend of ours, was coming off her midnight shift. The driver always parked as close as possible to the door of the building as it was always so dangerously cold that no one wanted to be outside for more than a couple of seconds. When he saw her coming, he jumped out and opened the door for her. On this particular night, she was just about to enter the vehicle when she caught a glimpse, out of the corner of her eye, of a polar bear cub, a huge animal even so, standing near the back of the vehicle. Nicky dove into the vehicle with such force that she went right out the other side knocking the driver off his feet as he was opening his door to re-enter. The startled bear sauntered off. And one day, a pilot friend of mine took me out bear watching. As we flew out over Hudson Bay near Eskimo

Point (now Arviat), we spotted 14 huge polar bears. This was probably not a good choice of recreational activity, I suppose, but it was an awe-inspiring sight, and we did get back to base without mishap. It is interesting to see that Fort Churchill and Polar Bear Viewing Expeditions are now a very popular and expensive tourist attraction, especially for Americans.

Something that did not seem so funny at the time but is somewhat laughable now were my occasional travels by town bus from the town site to the base. On many a dark morning, I and my fellow passengers, mostly Inuit people who worked on the base, had to get off the bus to push it in order to get it started. We still had to pay our full fare though. The bus seats were so cold it was almost impossible to sit on them, and the inside of the bus was usually coated with hoarfrost. The Inuit suggested that their ancestor's igloos had probably been much cozier. Most of the remaining igloos were well outside of the town of Churchill and many of the Inuit, who worked on the base, eventually moved there and lived in houses that were built by the Canadian government.

To make matters worse, in the winter it was dark pretty much around the clock. We went to work in the dark and came home in the dark. Of course, we made up for that in the summer because then it was light pretty much around the clock. Try going to sleep at night in that environment! Some other things were also unique to Fort Churchill, like having to tie two extremely scrawny Christmas trees together to make one very scrawny Christmas tree, and for one mediocre musician to be turned into a one-man band...the latter applying only to me.

The base commanding officer informed me that he was having a bugle flown in from Winnipeg so that the "General Salute" could be played on parades. He wanted everything in readiness when the Air Commodore arrived for his inspection. I was to be the bugler, never mind that I had never played a bugle nor did I ever want to play a bugle. "You're a musician," says he, "and you'll work it out." When the bugle arrived, it was a World War I something or other, not a bugle and not a trumpet as it had no valves. The Americans, who operated the First Arctic Test Centre where they tested their helicopters for winter conditions, took pity on me and they lent me a regular trumpet, so once I figured it out, everything worked fine. Then the commanding officer figured that, since I had done such a great job, he was going to get me a drum to go along with the trumpet. Whoop-dee-do! I was to be both trumpeter and drummer at the same time. I tried to tell him that, in such frigid weather, the trumpet would have to be kept warm or it wouldn't work, but to no avail.

At the next parade, with the Air Commodore, a famous Spitfire pilot from World War II, in attendance, I stood outside with my drum in hand and my trusty trumpet on a table beside me, completely nude – the trumpet, that is. The parade formed up inside the hanger and, on command, marched out to the beat of my drum, stopped in front of me, turned right – 15 paces to the drum beat, HALT, drum down, trumpet up...so far so good. Two toots; mouthpiece stuck to lip. No more sound...valves stuck...dead silence, the parade continued on without my participation, much to the embarrassment of the commanding officer who had tried so hard to impress the Air Commodore. My fellow airmen and I thought it rather amusing as I walked off the parade square with the frozen trumpet stuck to my lip. That night, as I played drums with my regular dance band at a dinner and dance in honour of the Air Commodore, he came up to the bandstand and said, "Aren't you the airman who messed up the parade today? I suggest from now on, you stick to your drumming. You're good at that. I'd stay away from that trumpet if I were you!" "YES SIR!"

After we had been in Fort Churchill a few months, I was sent to Winnipeg on a course. Ruby would be alone for the month or so that I would be away. This was particularly stressful for her, as the American couple who were our neighbours on one side had gone back to the States for the winter, and the neighbours on the other side had just been transferred out to Quebec. Although the main roads were usually cleared, as was the board-walk behind our house, the huge snow banks surrounding our house made it seem like we were living in a very deep valley. In addition it was so cold that the frost would build up on the hinges of the back door causing the door to pop open during the night.

Ruby used to have to get up and go to her teaching job when it was still dark. The town site of Churchill definitely had a criminal element because many people with questionable back-grounds had come from different parts of Canada to seek employment and they had brought their previous inclinations with them. There were incidents of rape, theft, drunkenness, bootlegging, stabbings, home invasion and general crimes. Consequently, it was not exactly ideal for Ruby to be living in Churchill on her own while I was away. The crazies in town were fond of tapping on the window or on the side of the house as they passed by on the boardwalk, a sidewalk made of boards that ran behind the houses connecting them up with the water line that ran from the priest's house to the CP water tank. Sometimes they would help themselves to the contents of our oil tank. One night, after deciding she had enough of the harassment, Ruby pulled on my Arctic parka, which completely enveloped her, and my flight boots and, with my 30/30 rifle in hand (no bullets), stepped outside. She did not get far as the culprits saw her coming and disappeared in a hurry. I guess she was probably more scared than they were. Her bedfellows, when she was home alone, were a hatchet, a hammer, and her trusty bulletless rifle and, if anyone did want to break in and do her harm, all the weapons to do the job were at hand! Not only did she have to deal with the tormentors who tapped on the house, she also had to deal with a gang of men living in a trailer, which was known as the tin shack, who would observe when I went to work on the midnight shift. Shortly after I would leave home and she had gone to bed, the phone would ring and on the other end a man's voice, sometimes a French voice with a bunch of wild noises in the background, would taunt her knowing that she was there alone. I reported it to the RCMP and they would drive by to check on her after that. I eventually figured out who was making the calls and one day I confronted the guy in the hangar and told him that if it happened again, I would beat the crap out of him. After that, it came to an end. Ruby survived the weeks on her own, but I have to agree with her that the townsite of Churchill was no place for a woman alone at that time.

Sometime around 1959 or early 1960, Anthony Quinn came to Fort Churchill to film a portion of his movie *The Savage Innocents*. He needed someone to drive him around and I volunteered. He might be a great actor, but he sure was a rotten tipper! I think I am still bitter about the fact that I drove him all around in our Buick and he did not even give me (or reportedly any of the staff at the hotels and restaurants) a tip. Speaking of our old 1957 Buick, we later took advantage of our American neighbour Smokey Smith's offer to store our car for the winter. The garage was barely big enough to get the car in. Sometime over the winter, the car shifted over the icy floor in the garage and froze into the ground and, in the spring, we were unable to get it out. Smokey who was, incidentally, the first American trapper to come to Churchill, said, "No problem, we'll just tear the garage down,"and we did.

After 24 months in Fort Churchill, we were transferred back to Ontario. We were happy to have had the experience of a northern posting but two years had been more than enough. It was great to be back in Trenton. Ruby again taught school (she was always able to find teaching work anyplace we lived), I was playing with a great band and then, in less than two years, a new posting came. This time, though, we did not mind as it was to One Fighter Wing, RCAF Marville, France, about 140 kilometres from Paris. We knew this meant we would be able to stay in one place for at least four years.

We first lived in the pleasant French town of Longuyon, with a beautiful view of the surrounding pastoral countryside from our living room window. It was during this time, in 1964, that our daughter Eydie (for Eydie Gormé) was born. Just down over the hill was a marketplace and a typical French market square, including a bakery where we used to go each morning to get a French baguette straight from the oven...some good! However, this particular part of Northeast France remained a stronghold of communist ideology and, as a result, Canadian and American forces were not too popular amongst most of the population. Some Frenchmen expressed their displeasure at our presence in their country by displaying such signs as, "Go home Americans and take your crazy Canadian friends with you!" A few years later, in 1966, De Gaulle would kick NATO troops out of France and, in 1967, One Wing Marville moved to Lahr, Germany. Some of the French were not long in forgetting that it was the Americans and Canadians, and Newfoundlanders aiding the British, that resulted in the liberation of their country. So much for gratitude!

Because of the challenges of living near the strong communist element in Longuyon, we sought and soon found a beautiful and very suitable brick and stone house in the Belgian country-side. We moved to a place called Dampicourt, just over the Belgian border, close enough that I could make the daily commute. It seemed very odd to us that many of the farmers there kept their animals close by in barns attached to their houses. It was not unusual to be sitting in the kitchen and to see a cow or two with its head over the door that separated the barn from the kitchen. Having the animals so near was certainly convenient for the farmers and, because they were spotlessly clean people, the smells associated with cattle were kept to a minimum and were not offensive to anyone.

Our Belgian landlords, a middle-aged couple who spoke only French, were the best of neighbours and they made us feel very much at home while we lived there. Shortly after we had arrived in France, I joined the RCAF Pipe and Drum Band as a drummer. I also joined up with five professional musicians and formed a dance band. (Yes, I still found time to work at my Air Force job.) The Pipe and Drum Band was so popular throughout Europe, especially in France, Belgium and Luxembourg, that we could only accept half the engagements we were offered. We used to go, with other military bands, to many large jamborees. No matter how outstanding the music was from some of the other bands, as soon as we made our appearance, sometimes even before we started to play, people came from everywhere. This was not because we were so musically superior or anything like that. I am sure that it was the distinctly different sound of the pipes, combined with drums, and the colourful kilts, tunics, spats and feather bonnets we wore that was the big attraction. Some of the most memorable places we played were le palais de Chaillot in Paris and Chateau Fontainebleau, a favourite retreat of Napoleon Bonaparte's, and which he had redecorated for his Empress Josephine, both magnificent! We also played at the schoolhouse in Reims where the Allies had accepted the terms of the surrender of the German High Command.

One very memorable incident took place during a parade held to commemorate General Patton's contribution to the World War II effort. The RCAF Pipe and Drum Band was in attendance. A part of the parade included a truck filled with Belgians who were Nazi sympathizers. They were dressed in Nazi uniforms and were giving the Nazi salute. Jake Langston, a piper with our band, a big, strong but normally gentle man, became so enraged he could not contain himself. He was a World War II veteran who had been shot down over Germany, captured and imprisoned for many months in German POW camps. He turned to me and said, "Frank, hold my pipes," and Jake went aboard that truck like a mad man. Belgians were flying everywhere. Jake's fellow band members managed to restrain him, but not before there were some very surprised and sore Belgian/German sympathizers that day.

As for the dance band, we wore crimson hats and jackets with gold crests and we called ourselves the Golden Knights. The sound we produced was so "awesome" (a word I have picked up from my young grandson, Joshua) and so popular that I considered denouncing my Canadian citizenship and staying in Belgium to continue playing with those fine musicians – Achilles Mahey (sax and clarinet), François (trumpet), François II (trumpet), another François who played violin, guitar and pretty much anything you handed him, and Gerard, who also played everything but mainly operated the ecophone, then yet another François who played piano, and Frank (moi) on drums. One month we played 36 gigs. However, my wife would not let me leave Canada behind. I think she said, "You're not doing that, my son, so you might as well get that out of your mind!" In all seriousness, this was one great band. We used to import the sheet music from London and Brussels (not that I could read a note), and play the most popular tunes of the day.

One evening, I was on my way from Belgium over the border into France to play at a dance when I suddenly felt a sickening thud. I jumped out of my 1956 Ford to see a bleeding woman lying beside the car's front fender. Achilles, who was sitting in the passenger seat, exclaimed, "Ooh la la François!" People came running from all over as I removed my band jacket and put it under her head. In a very short time, the ambulance and police arrived. I was shaking like never before in my life, at least not since wartime. I thought I had killed her, although the smell of liquor rising from her was enough to preserve her and came close to intoxicating me. The streets were so narrow in this part of Belgium, one could step off the curb right into the path of an oncoming car and, luckily, it was impossible to speed. I learned that this woman was the town drunk and this was not her first time being involved in an accident. Although her husband was trying to get at me with a tire iron, the police and the many onlookers concluded that I was not at fault, and they sent me on my way. I was one very distraught drummer that night with more drum rolls and trembles than usual. To console me, and after seeing all the blood on my clothes, the Roman Catholic Padre gave me a stiff drink of cognac. Not to be outdone, the Protestant Padre, Wilson Yeats, gave me an even bigger drink of cognac. After the drinks took effect, I did not care if I ran over all the old ladies in Belgium. Anyway, thankfully, my victim recovered from her injuries and, eventually, she graduated from crutches to a cane and returned to the streets, always flashing her toothless grin at me and waving her cane in welcome as I passed by…poor old thing! The custom guys on the border, who knew me quite well from my many trips, thereafter always jokingly referred to me as "Monsieur L'Assassin."

The byways and roadways in the French and Belgian country-sides were so narrow and dark that an accident was always waiting to happen. Monks, from a monastery on the road we used to take into France, often walked in the evenings and, as they were completely garbed in black, all one could see as they walked were the soles of their shoes. I always gave myself lots of travelling time and was very careful whenever I drove along these roads.

The Belgian town squares and marketplaces were enjoyable places to visit, and we often spent time strolling the old cobbled streets, visiting the interesting historic buildings and socializing with the locals. The colourful stacks of fruits and vegetables displayed in most marketplaces were a pleasure to behold. Incidentally, the *boucheries* always featured horse meat for sale, not that we ever purchased any! We used to frequent a little town called Florinville, not far from where we lived in

Dampicourt, and the specialty of one of the shops there was the best french fries ever, served with mayonnaise. We skipped the mayonnaise but many other Canadians and Americans learned to like the odd combination. Still, we didn't find the french fries quite delectable once we learned that they were cooked in 75 percent horse fat.

My main reason for wanting a posting to France was to have the opportunity to revisit as many places associated with my wartime service in Europe as we possibly could. With that in mind, the place we started with was The Battle of the Bulge area in Belgium, going first to Malmedy, the site of the Malmedy Massacre. As I stood at the base of the monument, on which were recorded the names of the 84 brave American soldiers who had been murdered there, it was hard to contain the flood of emotions that swept over me. I could almost see the weather conditions at that time, the same here as they were where we were fighting only a few miles away. It was cold and snowy with mud everywhere and the ground splattered with the blood of slain American prisoners of war. The news of the massacre had spread quickly to our regiment, but the enormity of what happened was not fully revealed to me until the story of one of the survivors, Staff Sergeant Bill Merriken, surfaced years later.

On December 17, 1944, the SS commander Joachim Peiper came upon a company of 30 or so trucks carrying American soldiers from the 285th Field Artillery Battalion. They were moving toward Malmedy. Peiper's tanks opened fire on the battalion and, as shells exploded around them, the Americans abandoned their vehicles and ran for cover. When the firing stopped, the Americans were rounded up and taken prisoner. This was bad enough, but at least they were still alive.

However, the Germans then herded Merriken and about 120 men, including medics and some military policemen, into a field where they stood with their hands over their heads. Two other German tanks arrived on the scene and they were ordered to cover the prisoners with their machine guns. Later reports indicated that some of the Americans may have tried to escape into the surrounding woods, when, Merriken said, suddenly one German officer shot one of the American soldiers, and then all the prisoners were mown down under a hail of machine gun fire. When that stopped, the Germans went through the field, pistols ready for any survivors they found.

Merriken had been shot twice and had lain beneath dead or dying fellow soldiers while the Germans, for at least a minute, walked around spraying them with bullets whenever they spied a twitching body or a wisp of vapour rising into the air around a soldier who obviously was still breathing. Merriken lay face down in the mud when a shot was fired above him, went through a body or bodies on top of him and hit him in his right knee. Despite the pain, he managed to remain still. When it seemed quiet, he crawled out and saw some other soldiers emerge, too. But so did the Germans, who starting firing again. Merriken managed to evade this and found shelter in a shed, where he passed out, and the next day was discovered by another American soldier trying to get back to American lines. The two were able to crawl and claw their way to a Belgian farmhouse, some distance away, where they were taken in, hidden and cared for until they were able to reach their regiment. Miraculously, 43 American GIs survived. But 84 bodies were left in the snow.

As I stood there at the monument recalling the story as it was relayed to us, I wondered about Peiper, the author of such butchery. He survived the war, and was tried at Dachau in 1946, found guilty of war crimes and sentenced to hang. However this was eventually commuted and he was released in December 1956. For the next decade or so he was involved with the German car industry, and then retired to France in 1972. But his wartime actions continued to cast a shadow. In July 1976 an unidentified group opened gunfire on his house and tossed Molotov Cocktails. His body was found in the charred remains. No charges were ever laid. Going back to Malmedy, and recalling the details of the massacre there, seemed almost unreal. This peaceful seemingly unscathed area, just 22 years ago, had been the setting for the vile action that had resulted in the senseless murder of so many young men, some of them still teenagers.

Our next trip into what had been the Belgian war zone was to Bastogne, close to Malmedy. This was where our 59th Newfoundland Heavy Regiment had fought so valiantly and where the Allies, in the face of such great odds, had been victorious over the Germans. In the town's square, which was renamed to honour General McAuliffe, on a mound, sat a World War II American Sherman tank with an 88 mm shell hole in its turret. The shell had penetrated three to four inches of solid steel and had killed the tank commander and his crew. These were vivid reminders of McAuliffe's brave response to the Germans' demand for surrender: "NUTS." The Germans soon discovered what this meant. The outcome of that exchange between the Germans and the Allies under McAuliffe could have been devastating, but instead we won the victory and it was, as some suggested, instrumental in changing the course of the war in Europe. In Bastogne, we also visited General McAuliffe's Museum with its relics and documents of the battles fought in the Bulge area.

It is difficult to remember or to describe much of what we experienced in Bastogne in 1944. I do recall the terrible winter weather with its snow, winds and frigid temperatures, and wondering if we'd ever again experience warmth. I remember too that the battles were unbelievably fierce, the outcome of most of them unpredictable, and the pain and brutality inflicted upon human beings by other human beings unforgettable. Of course, the horrors of war had confronted us since we first landed at Caen, but to a much lesser degree. Here at Bastogne, there had been a vast accumulation of troops and weaponry on both sides, ready to fight to the death, determined to win, at whatever cost.

I remember specifically when we first began to observe the results of conflict. It was just outside of Caen, I believe, when two of our battery soldiers were injured and were what one then called "shell shocked." They had to be returned to a medical facility, and eventually home, one to Newfoundland and one to England. It's not that incidents of injury and death became of any less significance to us, but by the time we were involved in the Battle of the Bulge, we had seen so much that we had become somewhat desensitized and could tolerate things more easily.

After living in Belgium for a year, we moved back to France, and we spent much of the next three years travelling to many places throughout Europe that we would never have had the opportunity to visit were it not for this posting. We went to

Italy, Spain, Switzerland, Austria, Germany, Luxembourg and Holland. We drove through southern France once and, in crossing over the Pyrenees Mountains, decided to visit the Principality of Andorra. We drove up into the mountains over the narrowest of roads with terrifying hairpin turns, squeezing even closer to the edge in order to pass men leading heavily laden donkeys along the roadways. I didn't see any place where I could turn around so we had to keep on going, wishing we were as nimble as the mountain goats we could sometimes get a glimpse of through the clouds. We felt sure it was only a matter of time before we would have to abandon the car and walk. However, once we got to Andorra, on the mountaintop, we had the most magnificent view imaginable. Brooks were babbling all over. I never saw anything like it in my whole life. The air was clean, clear and energizing and it was well worth the nerve-shattering expedition up the mountain. We stayed in Andorra longer than we had intended to. I don't remember if it was because we liked it that much, or if we were just too afraid to drive back down again.

One scene that remains in my mind is the one that confronted us one evening as we were driving along at the base of the Pyrenees. We had just left Limoges, famous for its beautiful bone china, and we were planning to drive for another hour or so to reach our accommodations for the night. A misty rain was falling, and blankets of fog came rolling in, making it difficult to see the road. Suddenly, we seemed to be transported back to medieval times. A very old, majestic stone castle appeared out of the mist and fog. It was perched high atop a hill and appeared to be still guarding the ancient city of Foix. The time of day, the fog, and the rain all together created a very eerie feeling. It was not a place for lingering, and we moved along until we were out of the fog and at our destination for the night. As our journey continued, we were able to have short visits at Saint-Tropez, Nice and Monte Carlo, all of which are in the south of France, and then from there to Genoa, Italy. We were particularly interested in Genoa because, as we had learned in school, it was the home of John Cabot who in 1497 discovered our beloved Newfoundland. We moved on to Venice where St. Mark's Square, with its flocks of pigeons, the canals and taxis (boat rides) around the city and the gondolas all added to the romance of the place. We then continued on to Monaco on the Italian Riviera, the French Riviera and then on to the beaches of Barcelona in Spain. It was all quite exciting for us and we wonder now where we got the energy for so much travel.

One country we visited frequently was Holland. We used to go to Eindhoven or to Maastricht to shop. The Dutch people, as soon as they discovered we were Canadians, could not do enough for us. They credited us with saving their country from the Germans and, for some reason, seemed to prefer us to the Americans. I don't know why, they just did. It was rewarding to be able to drive over the dam that holds back the North Sea, into the clean, wholesome, restored country, which had been so ravaged during the war years. We visited the zoos and museums, the waterways of Amsterdam and Rotterdam, and we marvelled at the fields of tulips and other flowers in The Hague, and practically all over Holland. A favourite place for us and for other people with children to visit was the miniature village of Madurodam, a perfect duplicate of a Dutch town with everything scaled down to child size, an amazing creation by some very talented people.

It was a great disappointment to me that time and circumstances did not permit me to revisit the beaches of Normandy where we had landed in 1944, specifically at Juno Beach. I was gratified, however, when my daughter, Eydie, was able to go to Omaha Beach a few years ago, as a French interpreter and a representative of the American Salvation Army. She and her husband and some of the Salvation Army staff catered and ministered to the large number of World War II Veterans who were there for commemoration ceremonies. They were overwhelmed by the many vets who stopped by for donuts and coffee and to share stories of the part the Salvation Army had played in their lives while they were in England and all throughout Europe. I suppose a little is always much when it in any way alleviates human suffering.

This is illustrated by a story told by Dr. Charlie O'Connell, and passed on to me by his brother John, a good friend of mine. Their father had been a medical officer during World War I. Captain O'Connell told his sons of how he had been in the trenches hour after hour, day after day, while the enemy delivered a series of deadly attacks. One day, he had attended so many wounded and dying, and had observed so many already dead, that his body and his spirit were broken to the extent that he was on the verge of collapse. He felt a hand on his shoulder. He looked up to see a man in a Salvation Army uniform, a smile on his face, a canteen of tea on his back, and a box of buns in his hand as he said, "Would you like a cuppa and a bun, Captain?" The compassion of that Salvation Army officer, in that horrible trench where he did not need to be, only wanting to be of service to his fellow man in whatever little way he could be, deeply affected Captain O'Connell. He respected and helped the Salvation Army whenever he could for the remainder of his life. After the war, he became a doctor and dedicated his life to his fellow citizens in the Bay of Islands. He was well regarded and loved by all who knew him. A long time care facility in Corner Brook is dedicated to him and named in his honour, as is a highway, O'Connell Drive, in the Bay of Islands area.

When Eydie and the Salvation Army entourage left the D-Day celebration, the streets from Normandy, almost to Paris, were lined with French people, old and young alike. They filled both sides of the streets waving American and Canadian flags to honour the Veterans of D-Day and World War II. For Eydie, it was all very emotional especially knowing that her dad had been a part of it all.

On a return trip from Italy, on one occasion, we journeyed through the Alps and down into Innsbruck, Austria. After our visit there, we went to Germany to a place near Munich. Throughout Europe, during the war, there were a number of concentration camps which Hitler had set up as extermination centres for Jews and other people whom he considered to be inferior beings. In all, over six million Jews, and countless numbers of people of other races, were exterminated. Three of the most infamous camps were Auschwitz in Poland, and Buchenwald and Dachau in Germany. Many of the Jews and others, men, women and children, went straight from the railway cars, which brought them there, to the gas chambers at one of these or at other camps. Other prisoners, being considered strong enough to be put to work, were spared. They were merely beaten, stripped naked, shaved of all head and body hair, and left cold and hungry to stand outside in bitterly cold weather, never knowing if and when they would be selected for extermination. If they were allowed to go inside, they were housed in squalid conditions, like hens in filthy coops. Outside, they were kept in barbed-wire enclosures, and while thousands died, some did manage to survive these horrific conditions. Our destination, at this particular time, was Dachau and, as we viewed the showers that had been used as gas chambers, and the ovens that had been used as crematoriums, we again marvelled at man's inhumanity to man. It is hard to come to terms with the evil of which man is capable, but especially in times of war, it is all too evident. So much has been written about the horrors of these camps that I need not relate more. Suffice it to say, Dachau and other such camps need to be kept alive in people's minds in order to prevent such atrocities from ever happening again. It was in a very sombre mood that we departed Dachau, but thanking God that the Allied Forces had been given the ability to destroy at least one evil regime.

By the way, thinking back, I don't recall hearing anything about the presence of extermination camps while the war was going on in Europe. I do remember though, passing through a little town or village in Holland, a place called Vught, and seeing there a gigantic accumulation of what appeared to be used clothing, including piles of boots and shoes in many sizes and in various degrees of decay. Some of us wondered, at the time, how and why it happened to be there, and now I wonder if it had any connection to the dreadful death camps.

During the time we lived in France, we used to shop at the American Post Exchanges in Etain and Verdun. Verdun is well known in military circles because it was the site of some of the most bitter fighting of World War I between the French and the Germans. The contents of the basement of the Ossuary in Verdun confirmed this as the skeletons of hundreds, possibly of thousands of French soldiers were stored there. We viewed this gruesome sight only through the Ossuary windows, a ghastly scene indeed. The most disturbing, I think, was seeing so many human skulls stacked or thrown together in one section of the Ossuary's basement. We also went to visit the two military cemeteries in the vicinity of Verdun, and we could only imagine the ferocious fighting that had caused them to be filled with thousands of slain French and German soldiers. What a sight were those hosts of white crosses, row on row, as far as the eye could see. Large sections of land in the Verdun area, to this day, are roped off because of the danger of unexploded shells from World War I, another testament to the futility of war.

Visiting Verdun brought back memories about a few incidents that had occurred in the Falaise Gap when our 59th Newfoundland Heavy Regiment was engaging the Germans there. One involved two young German soldiers, members of the Hitler Youth. In the midst of a pitched battle, which the Germans were losing, they jumped into a slit trench. Nothing could persuade them to throw out their weapons and surrender. Eventually, since we could not leave them there to do God only knows what when the opportunity arose, an Allied soldier reluctantly tossed a hand grenade into the trench. What a senseless loss of young life, and yet another atrocity!

At another time, a concrete German bunker on top of hill 112 was posing a huge problem for the Allies. The height of the hill and the strategic location of the bunker was allowing the Germans to cover a vast area, and to pin down the Allied troops – in this case our battery, #22. The six-barrel *Nebelwerfers* lobbed shells, which we referred to as "Moaning Minnies" because of the sounds they made, from the hill in the direction of our battery. They exploded immediately upon touching the ground, and sent out shrapnel horizontally to ankle depth. These were deadly, short-range weapons and we were in a most precarious situation until our big guns, with their 200-pound shells, established the proper range and zeroed in on the bunker. Then it was all over for the Germans and their Moaning Minnies, another reason to thank God that we had the most powerful guns of World War II.

Something more amusing happened when a soldier from our regiment, sitting over the hole of an improvised toilet with a burlap enclosure, heard someone in a voice not much louder than a whisper say, "*Nicht ein Nazi.*" A hand appeared holding a white rag and a rifle was thrown on the ground not far from the soldier's feet. Obviously, the "surrenderer" was a reluctant soldier of the German Army, a young man from a German-defeated country – in this case, Poland – who had been forced, like so many others, to fight with the Germans. Whenever they had the opportunity to do so, many of them surrendered to the Allies and became, in what they considered to be a better deal, Allied prisoners of war.

Speaking of the *Nebelwerfers* that the Germans loved to use against us brings to mind another weapon the Germans acquired late in the war. It was a German fighter plane, identified as the *ME 262*, which was the first jet fighter to be used during the war. It was 130 mph faster than anything the Allies had. Some historians believe that if the Germans had had a sufficient number of these jet fighters, and if they could have used them early in the conflict, it would have had a profound impact upon the duration of the war, probably prolonging it considerably.

Despite the World War II destruction of Europe's great edifices, there were still many cathedrals, museums and other structures that were splendid to visit, and we took advantage of as many as we possibly could before our posting to France came to an end. One of our last trips of significance was a final visit to Paris. The manager of the base garage in Marville asked me if I had ever driven my own car in Paris, or if someone else had been the driver. When I answered to the latter, he informed me that Paris was a very difficult city to navigate, and that in spite of his being a *Parisien* and used to driving there all his life, it took him three days one time to exit the Arc de Triomphe. I am sure that was a tongue in cheek statement, but I was gullible enough to park my car in the suburbs and take a taxi into the city.

We did the usual "touristy" things such as visiting the Eiffel Tower, the Louvre, Napoleon's Tomb, the Cathedral of Notre Dame, the Palais de Versailles and other places of interest. Since I had not driven my own car into the city, we had no trouble exiting the Arc de Triomphe at the end of our tour. In 1967 our stint in Europe came to an end and we returned to Canada with a posting to Ottawa.

We quickly adapted to that beautiful capital. My wife returned to school teaching, our daughter was happy with her new life and I became a member of the Capital Jazz Band. I later moved on to the Grey Jazz Big Band, as my hair became greyer and greyer, so all was well! We expected another round of these short two-year postings, but we were able to spend the next five years in Ottawa until I retired, at the compulsory age for my rank, in 1972. It was my intention to find a nice, interesting job, and to remain in Ottawa. However, as I was still somewhat infected with wanderlust and, since the opportunity presented itself almost immediately upon my retirement, I accepted a position with the Department of External Affairs.

I anticipated being in Ottawa for several months, but because I had had Top Secret Security Clearance while serving with the RCAF, my documents were processed very quickly, and we headed out to Moscow, USSR. After spending a few pleasant days in London, England, we boarded British Airways, thankful that it was not Russian Aeroflot. We had heard so many negative stories about Aeroflot that we were not anxious to patronize that airline. After a few hours we arrived in Moscow to begin our Communist Regime experience.

We knew when we arrived at Sheremetyevo Airport that living in this country was going to be a completely new experience. This was during the time when the USSR and the Western World were at loggerheads over the Anti-Ballistic Missile Treaty negotiations. We did not go directly to the airport terminal but were met, on the tarmac, about a mile away, by a bus complete with armed militiamen. Our passports, red, green and blue, according to one's status, were examined in that order, or to be more accurate, over-examined, and then we were taken to the terminal, still accompanied by our guards. Our bags were opened and inspected, with Canadian bags not being checked nearly as thoroughly as were those of the Americans. Our bags were merely riffled through while the Americans' were emptied out and every item was carefully scrutinized.

We were finally cleared and were at liberty to meet our hosts. I received a little shock here as I thought for a minute that Vladimir Lenin himself had come to meet me. The similarity was astounding as his colouring and stature, according to pictures I had seen of Lenin, were very similar, and I think he had taken great pains to acquire the similarly trimmed beard, the same glasses, etc. I don't know if he really admired Lenin on some fundamental level, or if he just wanted to garner some kind of weird attention for himself. Anyway, perhaps I listened all the more intently to his counsel on the way from the airport to our flat, feeling that I was in the presence of a great leader. I had been thoroughly briefed before leaving Ottawa, but my host further restated the importance of saying nothing of any significance once we entered our flat, because our flat was certainly bugged, and he wasn't referring to the cockroaches, which we discovered later were also in residence in most apartments. He also told me to be prepared for a comprehensive briefing at the embassy first thing in the morning.

Everything I had learned about Moscow before going there led me to believe that it was a beautiful old city. It was indeed an old city and in many respects a beautiful one, but, unlike some other great cities, it had, at least until recent years, an air of oppression and apprehension over it. It was also a very crowded city with eight million people living in a 34-square-mile area when we arrived there in 1972. In 1969, or thereabouts, Moscow had become so crowded that an official restriction had to be put on further growth, and a satellite city built, about 25 miles outside of Moscow, to handle the overspill. It seemed to me that yet another satellite city would be in order as the streets were teeming with people all day long. This was partially due to the fact that few of the vast population owned cars, and they lived in such crowded conditions that they had no room to store food. This made it necessary for them to shop daily at the bread stores, the grocery stores, the marketplaces, etc. So the people were always out and about. Thousands of people were always either entering or exiting the public transport systems to travel to and from their places of employment. Sometimes, if we happened to be walking somewhere, we felt as if we were in the midst of a thundering herd.

The city of Moscow stands on the Moskva River which runs a 28-mile course through the city. This river handles a myriad of smaller craft while the Moscow ship canal, which runs north to the Volga River, channels all regular passenger, cargo and pleasure craft activities. Like the streets, the waterways are also a beehive of activity. The city has an inner and outer ring road and a green belt which surrounds Moscow and covers 70 miles. As well, the famous and beautiful Lenin Hills overlook the right bank of the Moskva River, and is the location of the 32-storey Lomonosov Moscow State University, which was founded in 1755 and is the oldest and largest university in Russia.

Moscow, known as the City of Statues, is also famous for its many monuments and historical sites. At one time, Moscow was home to at least 350 Orthodox churches, all elaborately decorated and ornamented. Most of these have now been turned into museums. Taking a stroll around the city and view-ing the many statues that honour Russia's prominent artists and intellectuals – Tolstoy and Dostoevsky, Tchaikovsky and Rachmaninoff – was inspiring. However, the numerous statues paying homage to former Communist leaders like Stalin were less stirring, to say the least. Eventually, the enlightened people of the USSR removed Stalin's statue from Red Square. Yet thousands queued up, day after day, at the mausoleum on Red Square, to view the embalmed body of Lenin, an incredible sight.

One cannot describe the sights of Moscow without giving the spotlight to the Kremlin, to Red Square and to St. Basil's

Cathedral. The Kremlin is a triangular-shaped fortress that began as a wooden structure in 1150. At that time, it was surrounded by a moat which, in a later century, was filled in. The Kremlin was improved upon over the years, going first to earthen walls, then to brick walls and towers and, finally, to stone walls and bastions. Inside its walls is the Palace of the Grand Duke, containing a superb collection of the Czar's treasures. As well there are several other palaces, monasteries, and administrative buildings, most of them built of stone. There are six gates leading out of the Kremlin, three leading to Red Square. The magnificent St. Basil's Cathedral stands in Red Square adjoining the Kremlin walls. It has nine chapels surrounded by domes and spires of various shapes and beautiful colours. We were awe-struck by its architecture and beauty. When we saw it in reality, we could hardly wait to go inside. But what a disappointment! We knew that changes had occurred but we did not expect to see it almost completely gutted and in the process of being turned into a museum, which it is today, a major tourist attraction.

A half ring of monastery fortresses once protected the approaches to Moscow, some of which still remain, one of the most famous being Novodevichy, which we, like most of our compatriots, made it a priority to visit, because many of Russia's Communist leaders are buried there. We were most interested in seeing the final resting places of Khrushchev and of Stalin's son Vasily. Novodevichy Church is now, like so many other famous structures, a museum.

Moscow has long been the cultural hub of Russia. This is quite evident as, no matter what time of the day or evening it is, long lines of people are awaiting entrance to the most frequented places: museums, the Lenin State Library (which is one of the three largest in the world), the cinemas (of which there are 120 in the city), the planetarium, the puppet theatre, the many art galleries, and two of the most important and popular places of all, the famous Bolshoi, the theatre of opera and ballet, and the Moscow Art Centre Hall. We felt fortunate to have had the opportunity to attend many cultural events, but more importantly the average Russian citizen, who in many waysis, or used to be, greatly underprivileged, was able to take advantage of everything that was available. The population was encouraged to become culturally savvy, and Moscow's fine and convenient transportation system in and all around the surrounding area was inexpensive enough, and the admission prices low enough to allow nearly everyone to take in the events of their choice. The patience of the Russian people to endure long lines is commendable. Of course, and I assume living conditions have improved considerably since we were there some years ago, at that time it was preferable for many Russians to be seated in a beautiful concert hall or in some other setting than to be spending the evenings crowded into a one-bedroom, or if one was especially fortunate, a two-bedroom apartment, with 10 to 12 other family members.

We asked Ella, our daughter's Russian piano teacher, why it was that even on the coldest winter days so many senior citizens, especially *Babushkas* (grandmothers), would be bundled up and sitting on park benches all over the city. She said it was to give a little privacy to the younger family members, to free up a little space for students doing their homework, and to help retain some measure of sanity for themselves.

Apart from the many cultural events, there were also plenty of venues for other types of activities. There is a spectacular zoo and a continuously performing circus which, until we saw Cirque du Soleil in Minneapolis, we thought could never be equaled in performance. Other attractions are a Botanical Garden, a hippodrome, indoor and outdoor sports arenas and Lenin Central Stadium, all world-class facilities. It's no stretch to say there is something to suit everyone's taste in Moscow! Our daughter took swimming lessons at the indoor/outdoor pool and, for some reason unknown to me, they used the outdoor pool all winter long. The swimming coaches and spectator parents would view the goings on bundled up in their warmest winter clothing, often with the snow falling on them, and watch the swimmers as they entered the pool from the inside, exiting through a divided curtain and out into a cloud of steam. The kids thought it was great fun. For those people who wanted to ice skate, Gorky Park was one of the many places providing a rink, and a favourite place for the kids. Often times, figure skating stars would come from the US and skate with the children from the American and Canadian embassies. Speaking of ice reminds me of the greatest hockey series in history, played between Team Canada and the USSR National Hockey Team. It took place in Moscow in September 1972, and we were there! Attending the series at Luzhniki Sports Palace was very exciting for us and for the 3,500 other Canadians who came to the event. The final game was a victory for the Canadians with Paul Henderson scoring the winning goal in the last 34 seconds. The Soviets referred to us and our American fans/friends as a bunch of hoodlums (in the Russian language it sounded even more disdainful) after our rambunctious reaction. We in turn thought the Soviet spectators were very weird sitting there so staid and sombre in their black suits and ties, with scowls to match. So much for different cultures! As a result of Canada's hard won triumph over the USSR National Team, Luzhniki Sports Palace is probably better known to Canadians, at least to hockey fans, than is the Bolshoi Theatre.

Over the centuries, Russia has experienced so many disasters that a less resilient people and country might have succumbed, but, in spite of it all, it is amazing to see what Russia, especially the city of Moscow, has become today. Moscow was completely destroyed by fire at least four times, and the country had to deal with numerous raids from outside forces, most of them coming from the Cossacks and Tartars, the fierce fighting hordes from the Crimean area. Tyranny was always rampant within Russia, and revolutions and civil unrest were an ongoing part of the scenario. Since the early 19th century Russia has been engaged in three major wars: in the War of 1812 in which the French, under Napoleon, tried to occupy Russia by entering Moscow, and later in World Wars I and II.

While we, the 59th Newfoundland Heavy Artillery Regiment, were fighting at the Falaise Gap in France, we were well aware of the Russian's participation against Germany. They had already taken enormous losses, especially in 1941 when the German invaders were within 25 miles of Moscow; Moscow was in a state of siege and was being bombarded by German aircraft while terrible fighting raged all throughout the countryside before the Russians were finally able to mount a tremendous counterattack. And here we were in Moscow, some 30 years later, marvelling at its sights. Many of the beautiful old buildings, like the Ukraine Hotel, were still standing. There were amazing colourful onion domes and spires throughout the city, wide and well-appointed streets and a fabulous transit system.

One of the most amazing aspects of modern-day Moscow is the metro electric underground line, started in 1930 and serving at least 50 stations when we were there. The most striking element of the system, at least to us from the Western world, was the highly elaborate décor of the underground stations. It was like stepping into high-end art galleries, truly magnificent.

Back to our arrival in Moscow; I did receive my comprehensive briefing at the Canadian Embassy, as promised by Lenin's doppelganger, and I also acquired a supply of Russian currency in the form of rubles and kopeks, American currency in exchange for Canadian currency, and two books of coupons to be used at the Gastronome. The Gastronome was a store for personnel from the various embassies in Moscow, and for the Russian higher-ups, mostly military and government officials. There was usually a good supply of caviar, vodka and other alcoholic beverages. Speaking of vodka reminds me of a funny little incident. Our designated drivers, in their spare time, would wash our cars for us and, although they didn't ask for payment, they were always more than happy to accept a bottle of vodka. At this particular time, there were no large bottles of vodka at the Gastronome and, since the half-size bottles were in short supply, we presented our driver with only one smaller bottle, planning to make it up to him at a later date. We were surprised and amused when we discovered that only the bottom half of our car had been washed. Anyway, the Gastronome had a full stock of supplies which were luxuries to the Russians but, to us, apart from a few staples, inadequate to meet our needs. There was a good supply of beef if one's favourite cut was filet mignon. If we asked the Russian butcher for ground beef, he ground up filet mignon; oven roast, filet mignon; beef for soup, filet mignon. I couldn't have imagined getting tired of filet mignon but we did and, consequently, we ordered other cuts from Stockmann's, our source in Finland. Actually, we were never nutritionally deprived as all our staples and luxury European foods were brought in from Copenhagen, Denmark. We presented our orders to the embassy and, once every six weeks, we had a miniature Christmas when our cases of everything we liked best came in, usually with a few articles of clothing selected from the many catalogs they used to send us. Our milk came in from Helsinki, Finland, in half-gallon cartons that we kept in our freezer until they were needed. In Moscow, vegetables were limited in the winter to cabbages, beets and potatoes. As the fruits were mostly oranges and figs, we imported vegetables and fruits from Helsinki, adding a good supply of anything else we thought we were entitled to as our reward for living in Moscow. With our order, we would usually get a good quantity of gum and popcorn because our drivers, and our daughter's Russian teachers, would always request these items for their children. For people who enjoyed alcoholic beverages, and who hosted a lot of cocktail parties, there were lots of cases of various imported wines, beers and liquors. The reduced cost of these products to embassy personnel, and their easy availability, resulted in some people leaving the country complete with drinking problems. We didn't have wine racks or liquor cabinets in Moscow; we had liquor pantries stacked to capacity.

Moscow's bread stores are another story as there was always a good variety, especially if one liked the heavy rye and coarse-grained breads, but securing it required a lot of patience. First, there was usually a long line of customers waiting to get into the building. Once inside we were given a ticket with a number, after which we were at liberty to go to the racks and select our bread; you had better have a pencil with you to write down the number of your selection on your ticket. Next, you took your ticket to the cashier, who totalled up your purchase prices on an abacus, and you paid. Then you went back to the racks, picked up your bread and stood in line to exit the store, waiting your turn for the commissaire to check your purchase against her ticket. Then, voila, you were free at last, free to go home and eat!

There were several *berioskas* (shops that took only hard currency – not rubles) around the city with the same customer admissions stipulations as the Gastronomes, except for one day each month when they were open to all Russians employed at embassies who were in possession of coupons. These *berioskas* were also very popular with embassy people, each one having its own specialty. For those who wanted to buy well-crafted jewellery and perfumes, luxury clothing, electronics, and other fine products, the *berioskas* were the places to go, providing you didn't try on "open season days."

The apartment block in which we lived, on Kutuzovsky Prospekt, housed people from many embassies around the world. The entrance to the compound had a guardhouse manned by two or more armed militiamen. A second armed guardhouse stood in the middle of the compound facing the entrances to the apartment building. After being cleared to enter, it was then necessary to pass inspection by the Commissaire guarding one's particular entrance. Security was extremely tight, as it seemed to be wherever Americans were being housed...not sure if that was to provide them greater protection or greater surveillance. We were all watched very carefully, as I found out one day when our cat escaped from our apartment. A man in the guardhouse watched me try to catch the animal, and saw me go over the stone wall in pursuit. I caught our pet, but I was questioned and reprimanded by an armed guard before I was free to re-enter my apartment. He also informed me that I was "gloopy," a Russian word that wasn't meant to be complimentary, to put so much effort into recapturing a cat.

On our street, about half a mile from our flat, was the Museum-panorama of the Borodino Battle and the residence of the Russian Communist leader at the time, Leonid Breznev. His presence there was evident as every morning, promptly at 9:15, his car, with the curtains drawn and accompanied by his armed escort, went roaring down the *chaika* lane (one of the six lanes that was supposed to be for emergencies only) headed for the Kremlin where, undoubtly, he had important business to conduct.

About a month after our arrival in Moscow, in early July, we experienced record high temperatures. It was so hot that the numerous peat bogs around the city caught on fire. The stench in the air was a real health hazard for those with respiratory problems. It was also a problem for my wife who had had throat cancer a few years earlier. The doctors recommended she either return to Canada, or go to Helsinki, Finland, until the danger was over. She and our daughter chose Helsinki and spent the next ten days or so in that fine city.

We were to take several trips to Helsinki during the next two years, sometimes going there by Finnair, and other times by Russian train. Every time we travelled outside of city limits, it was necessary to get, through the embassy, a letter of permission indicating where we were going, why we were going, the length of our visit, and the name and address of the hotel in which we would be staying. Then we waited for the decision to be made. I don't remember ever being denied the certificate of travel, but I think to deal with our travel requirements, ankle bracelets might have been a better option.

Going from Moscow to Helsinki was somewhat similar to stepping out of the darkness into the light. The Finns were so friendly, at least in comparison to the Russians, and the shops, hotels and restaurants were so well appointed that it was a treat to spend time in the city. However, there were some things about the Finns that tipped my wife's opinion in favour of the Russians, at least as far as modesty was concerned. Ruby made regular visits to her doctor in Helsinki for cancer checkups, and the first time there, she undressed in the cubicle. When she couldn't locate a hospital gown, she requested one from the nurse, who said she didn't need one. She proceeded, with the nurse, to the doctor's office and was mortified to be shaking hands with the doctor while standing there stark naked. If the doctor had attempted to take her blood pressure then, it could have wrecked his machine. Later, we all went to a swimming pool, and we were a little surprised to see some pretty hefty naked women come out of the water, wrap a towel turban style around their heads, seat themselves at the poolside restaurant table and have a drink. Eydie hadn't seen this and came out in her swimsuit, dove into the pool, came up with eyes like saucers and said, "Let's get out of here. There are big naked women in there!" (Not knowing the language, we might have stumbled into a nudist colony.)

However, there were lots of other things to do and see that involved wearing clothes. Like most great cities, there was a variety of interesting museums and art galleries. There were bus tours of the city, tours of the waterways and visits to many marketplaces. There were specialty bazaars, one with mounds of beautiful flowers, another with all kinds of fruits and vegetables, one for arts, crafts and specialty clothing, another for meats and cheeses, plus many others and, our favourite of all, a dockside fish market. Although we were not big fans of fish while we were growing up in Newfoundland, we would soon develop a taste for it after we left the province...go figure! All this to say that Helsinki was so enjoyable we were always reluctant to return to captivity. I don't mean to suggest that Moscow was all gloom and doom; there were many, many things that we enjoyed, and we were treated to many luxuries. We were happy to have had the experience of Moscow, but the cloud of suspicion and apprehension that permeated everything sort of dampened the positive aspects of the city.

One trip we consider special was to Rovaniemi in Finnish Lapland. We left Moscow's railway station, got settled in our cabin without incident, and the steward brought us large glass cups of good Russian tea with jam as the sweetening agent, and biscuits and cakes. Then came the Inquisition. The guards requested our passports, asked a question or two, all very civil, bid us "dasvedanya" – good evening – and left, absolutely without stress for us. Then they went down the passageway where there were two cabins occupied by Americans. The mood changed completely. The Americans were asked to step out into the passageway; their magazines were confiscated and shaken out, their passports and wallets gone through, clothing thoroughly searched, and finally mattresses and bedding pulled out of the cabins and into the passageway. The only reason I can think of that would cause so much animosity towards the Americans by the Russians would be jealousy. Russia long yearned to be the world's superpower, and seemed to resent the fact that America was filling that role. Whether that was the motive or not, the Americans were often harassed without any apparent cause.

Once everything had settled down again, we continued on our journey. The train was clean and comfortable, and we were having a pleasant enough trip until we arrived at the border, to cross into Finland, at Leningrad. The train pulled into the station and policemen, armed with machine guns, were everywhere on the platform. The militiaman who had travelled with us on the train, together with the customs officials, guarded exits, and after they had examined again the documents of those ending their journey at Leningrad, and they had detrained, the armed policeman came on board, counted the number of empty seats against their roster, then left the train, locked the doors and went inside the train depot – to do their paperwork, I presume. Eventually, I suppose, they decided that since we were no threat to anything or anybody, we were cleared to proceed on our journey, and we reached Helsinki without further incident. We spent a day or two in Helsinki and then boarded a Finnish train to continue on to Rovaniemi, Lapland.

Lapland stretches across the northern area of Norway, Sweden, Finland and the USSR, and in Rovaniemi we were in the same latitude as Canada's Frobisher Bay on the Arctic Circle. I had occasion to go to Frobisher Bay in 1979 and, at that time, I couldn't help but compare the cleanliness and well laid out situation which I had observed in Rovaniemi with the dirty, untidy place that was Frobisher Bay. Frobisher Bay is under the jurisdiction of the Canadian government, it being one of several Canadian centres across northern Canada, and the population there was made up primarily of indigenous people with a mix of government employees necessary for the maintenance of the facilities there.

What were you doing in Frobisher Bay in 1979, you might ask? I was working on the semi-submersible rig, *Sedco 709*. We were drilling off Brevoort Island, close enough to Greenland to get our drinking water from there. The project turned out to be a labour in vain as we came up with a dry hole and, as a result, we left the area and went to Newfoundland. We were not sorry to depart Frobisher Bay, but we would miss the delectable fish we had become accustomed to eating. Arctic char was in abundance in that area and we got plenty of protein from that source. I should mention, before I backtrack to Rovaniemi, about another narrow escape I had while in Frobisher Bay.

The *Sedco 709* was my first experience on an oil rig, and I flew from Montréal to Frobisher Bay by Nordair. On the way up, a fellow passenger, drunk as a skunk, removed her mukluks and stuck her bare, stinky feet on the seat arm in front of her – mine! Great start! After deplaning at Frobisher Bay and taking a very deep breath of fresh air, I boarded the 20-passenger Twin Otter which would take us to Brevoort, the jump-off place for the rig. As I donned my survival suit in preparation for the flight, via helicopter, to the rig, I said to myself, "What in the hell am I doing here? I'm 59 years old and I really don't need this!" However, off I went.

On this job, the crew changed every 21 days – 21 days of working 12-hour shifts, then 21 days off. During one of these crew changes, going from the rig to Brevoort, I was asked if I would consider going out on a later flight, as the Captain had an emergency at home and wanted to be sure he had adequate time to make his connections. Of course I was happy to oblige and, as I was waiting for the next flight, the terrible news reached us...the outgoing plane had crashed as it attempted to land at Frobisher Bay and, unfortunately, everyone on board had been killed. That kind of incident leads me to believe that everyone has a predestined time to exit this world. I could be wrong, but I have had too many narrow escapes in my own life, even excluding the war years, to be able to explain my survival in any other way.

Now, back to the capital of Finnish Lapland, Rovaniemi. The weather was so-o-o cold when we arrived in late December, but it was a brisk, invigorating chill and, with the proper Northern clothing, quite tolerable. We were able to stand beside a kiosk, which was serving piping hot bratwurst, and to watch the spectacular display put on by the *aurora borealis*. We seemed to enjoy everything about this frigid land – the chalet where we stayed, the reindeer stew, and other Finnish dishes we were served, especially the bowls of bakeapples with cream. The Finns called these berries cloudberries but I think we Newfoundlanders should know bakeapples when we see them. The gift shops offered a wide variety of bakeapple products for sale, including liqueur strong enough to knock your socks off, or so I'm told! As we travelled on the train from Helsinki, we had seen miles of marshlands covered with the yellow of bakeapples, a very pretty sight; I had never seen them in such abundance in Newfoundland.

Incidentally, if anyone is ever in need of a driver for a reindeer team, my wife, daughter and I are available as we have our reindeer driving licenses. (We haven't been able to have them renewed since we returned to Canada, however.) It was amusing to see the normally dressed Laplanders head for the reindeer stables to don their traditional garb when tourist buses were due in. The visitors were cordially welcomed, given a list of interesting events in which to participate and encouraged to get their reindeer driver's license. Our instruction lasted about 20 minutes. We did our trial run, received our documents and were assigned our team. Our run was about two miles, during which time the reindeer dumped us off a couple of times and, when we turned around at the end of the course, the reindeer took off for the stable, much faster than they had gone out, to indulge in their reward treats for catering to a bunch of foolish visitors.

We arrived back in Moscow in the midst of a heavy snowstorm. The city had a huge fleet of heavy equipment for snow clearing. They managed to keep the main streets reasonably clean, although the equipment was rather primitive, but manual labour was used for most of the other areas. We were often awakened before daylight as crews of workers, mostly women, used ice chisels and heavy brooms to remove ice and snow from the entrances and parking lots of the apartment building compound.

Our lives proceeded routinely for the remainder of the winter. We made a few weekend trips, with other embassy families, to the Russian country estates, the *dachas*, where there were ice skating rinks, *troika* rides and saunas to enjoy. At home, we went to church on Sunday mornings. One Sunday we would worship at the British Embassy which, except for the high church of England style of service, was more like attending an elite club where we sat on soft leather chairs and sofas in luxurious surroundings, and were served refreshments by snooty stewards. Talk about being out of one's league, that was us, although not so our daughter; she was young enough to accept it all as normal living. Every other Sunday, we went to the American Ambassador's residence for service; this was also quite classy but with a less formal worship service and in a more relaxed and friendly atmosphere. At both places of worship, the entrances were always guarded by militiamen...potentially dangerous people, these Christians!

As mentioned previously, after the 1917 Russian Revolution most churches in Moscow had either been eradicated or converted into museums and warehouses. However, people's desire for religious devotion had not been destroyed as, throughout the country, many Christians had gone under-ground and worshipped in designated homes in their neighbourhoods. Three churches, considered to be working churches, were opened while we were in Moscow. One of these was a large Baptist Church, where Billy Graham and his entourage came to conduct a series of prayer services. Interspersed with the hundreds of people attending the meetings were a number of uniformed Russian soldiers, under government orders to monitor the proceedings. The service I attended was very emotional as there were many older Russians there who were overjoyed to be able to worship in such an environment, regardless of the presence of the soldiers. A choir of approximately 50 to 60 people, led by a member of the Bolshoi Theatre, provided magnificent singing. A rendition of the old, well-known Christian hymn, "Blessed Assurance," was sung with such gusto and seemingly heart-felt emotion that I could hardly believe I was worshipping in a church in Moscow. I recall one time having three or four *dooniks* (Russian workers) doing some work in our apartment while I was playing a few tunes on the organ, mostly hymns I had learned growing up and attending church in the Salvation Army, one of which was "Blessed Assurance." The oldest gentleman was listening intently, sitting in an armchair rather than doing his work, with a big smile on his face. After several minutes I glanced at him and was surprised to see tears streaming down his face. He said, "*Monoga goda nazad, babushka,*" or "Many years ago, grandmother," which I took to mean his ancestors had been Christians and had sung these or similar hymns. I asked him if he was a Christian and where he worshipped. With his hand over his heart, in his halting English and with the help of his cohorts, he said that God was in his heart and he worshipped him always wherever he was.

Outside of Moscow, in a place called Zagorsk, there was a seminary operated by the Orthodox Church, and tolerated, but under the very strict discipline of the Russian government. My wife and three other women from the Embassy were asked to go there to present some books and other mementos from the Canadian government. Although the women were transported there in an Embassy limousine with a Russian driver and were carrying their passports and travel documents, they were thoroughly screened upon arrival, followed, and constantly photographed while they were on tour. It was a most interesting and educational trip for them, but the whole experience was somewhat intimidating. The Russians always made sure we knew who was in charge of all our activities.

Our daughter Eydie attended the Anglo-American school in Moscow, together with pupils from 31 different embassies. British and American teachers, plus a smattering of special subject Russian teachers, made up the staff. Russian was taught in school and, because children seem to have an aptitude for language, they were soon able to communicate with each other in that language. Eydie had arrived in Moscow in June and, by the time she started school in September, she already had a fair Russian vocabulary because of her interaction with other children in the compound. I had a private Russian teacher but found the language much more difficult to learn than French, which I had studied, and mastered somewhat, while in the Royal Canadian Air Force. It doesn't really matter much about either of these now, because I've gone back to speaking nothing but Newfoundlandese.

The American, British and Canadian embassies did a fine job of providing the children of embassy personnel with the best of entertainment and the opportunity to attend all sorts of cultural events. The time spent in Russia was a great learning experience for the kids although there was a danger that such privileged living might instill in them a sense of entitlement which, when embassy life came to an end, could be difficult for some to overcome. Of course, not all the embassies catered so much to personnel or to their children, but many did. Embassy staff also enjoyed many perks such as the low cost of employing locals as housekeepers and cooks which freed up time for more interesting activities. The kids had Russian drivers to transport them to and from school, and they had enough activities to keep them occupied while the adults were able to attend dinner and cocktail parties and many other social and cultural events. Daytime bridge games were a favourite pastime, and so was the tasting of the variety of imported wines that were available. There were outdoor pursuits as well: ice skating, attending hockey games played by the male embassy members, etc. In many ways, it was an interesting enough life in a country that was oppressive enough, and depressing enough, to have our posting there classified as a hardship posting.

Speaking of dinner parties reminds me of a dinner given for us by Eydie's Russian piano teacher, Ella. She wanted to do something nice for us in appreciation for gifts we had brought her from one of our trips to Finland; that "great" gift was a Beatles record and a pacifier for the baby she was expecting – a very modest request she had made of us. Ella decided she would cook us a special dinner. She couldn't do it at her apartment because, not only was it too small for entertaining, it had no oven. This, in spite of the fact that she was a well-educated woman, a concert pianist and, if not a member of the KGB at least an informant for them. It took her several days to gather the necessary ingredients. One day she brought a chicken, which she stored in our refrigerator. The next day she brought beets to make Russian soup or borscht. Another day she brought cabbage, carrots and potatoes and, finally, on another day, and at another market, she found raw almonds, which she ground by hand, and some type of dried fruit, which she combined with the almonds and made into a cake that she served with Russian yogurt. The end result was a very good meal, but imagine all the effort put into the preparation of such a simple affair. However, she was so happy to do it, and we were certainly appreciative of her efforts.

Ella was a very nice person but, like most Russians we met, probably a little overzealous in her pursuit of perfection, both in herself and in her music students. One day, she became quite upset because Eydie hadn't practiced enough for a piece she was to play at an upcoming recital. After scolding her quite soundly, she went into a tirade to say, "If you were a Russian student, with your talent, you would be placed in a special music school where you would be expected to excel in music and also in academics. All this would be done, away from your parents." She accented her comments by telling Eydie that she was too pampered, which wasn't far from the truth, and by giving her a little tap with a pointer, on her fingers. I, being upset myself, informed her that in Canada we didn't think that way, and we were more concerned with seeing a child develop into a well-rounded human being, with many interests, while living with her parents; there were a few other civil comments after which Ella profusely apologized and cried, along with Eydie. Thank God she didn't decide to cook us another dinner as a further means of apology!

Looking back on our time in Moscow, and recalling how much effort it took for Ella to prepare her lovely meal, I can't help but think about how different things must be for Ella's daughter who was born the last year we were there, 1974. She has grown up, in large part, in the new and improved Moscow – a modern city comparable to any other large city of its size with a population of approximately eight million people, a city with contemporary and adequate housing for a large percentage of its inhabitants. There are big supermarkets, department and clothing stores, high-end fashion boutiques, trendy hotels and restaurants. Moscovites today can even indulge in fast foods, if they so desire, at one of the McDonald's establishments in the city. Also, I remember how excited Ella was to receive the gift of a Beatles record she had long craved. With Russia today being a more open society, her daughter might have been one of the thousands who attended the Paul McCartney: *Live in Red Square* concerts in 2003. Quite a change in the space of 20 years.

One day during our visit, the Canadian and British embassy personnel were invited to the Kremlin to take a tour of St. Michael's Castle and of the residence of the Imperial Family. Some details have now faded into oblivion, but I do recall the grandeur of these palaces, and the multitude of precious treasures contained therein. While the splendour of it all was almost intoxicating, there was also an element of disgust to think that human beings could go to such lengths to indulge their incredible egos. Little wonder Russia experienced so much social unrest and went through at least two great revolutions when there was so much disparity between the working man and the ruling regime.

I must describe, to the best of my ability, the excess of wealth that was evident in the Emperor's residence and also in the Empress's, adjoining. The windows and wallcoverings were of the finest silk, embossed with intricate designs and patterns, all in beautiful subdued colors; the crystal chandeliers glittered, not only with crystal but also with gold, silver and precious stones. The doorknobs were made of gold; gold and silver candlesticks adorned the already elaborately carved piano, and were placed in alcoves on pedestals and various scattered tables throughout the palaces; the fireplaces were fronted with richly coloured mosaic tiles and studded with various coloured stones; and all kinds of treasured paintings, sculptures, and wall hangings were in abundance. What I remember most vividly was a large black onyx table in the Empress's quarters, with inset flowers made of all sorts and sizes of diamonds, pearls, rubies and other precious gems covering the entire tabletop. A large gold clock was also in this room, and it was ablaze with coloured stones.

While the magnificence of the palaces was certainly awe-inspiring, there was nothing substantial or inspirational about it, as it was merely an example of incredible greed, and of man's total disregard for his fellow man. In today's world, it seems as if the wealthy, who spend billions of dollars to self-indulge in every way imaginable, are guilty of engaging in the same vulgarities as did the ruling classes of countries like Russia, acquiring wealth on the backs of others, through whatever means available, not necessarily honourable or legitimate. The end result is usually tragedy, as in the case of Czar Nicholas II, who with his wife Alexandra and five children was executed amidst the revolutionary turmoil of 1918.

In 1973, the Russians issued an invitation to members of the diplomatic corps to a special one-day event where they would be permitted to buy Russian icons and other valuable para-phernalia which were usually not for sale. Our purchases would be registered and documents issued allowing us to take the items out of the country duty-free. I was pleased to be able to purchase a solid brass portable icon depicting historical religious events, and a special silver ruble struck in 1896, to commemo-rate the visit of Czar Nicholas II to Leningrad. In hindsight, I think the Russians used us to rid themselves of religious items and relics of the Romanov reign which they no longer wanted in their country.

On some levels Moscow was, without doubt, a disheartening

city, but the parade that took place there to commemorate the 1917 Russian Revolution was downright frightening. As we stood in the Spasskaya Tower area of the Kremlin, with thousands of other spectators, we were mesmerized at the portrayal of the military might of the USSR. The procession began with thousands of people from the young pioneer group and many others from various parts of the communist system bearing flags, which turned the wide streets into a vast sea of red. This spectacle was followed with a massive display of personnel, from all branches of the military, synchronized like puppets on a string, with thousands of troops moving in a manner similar to that seen in parades out of North Korea and China. The impressive Red Army Band, interspersed with various other musical groups, was prominently placed next to the troops. What was most disturbing, even to those of us who had experienced war, was the array of military might in the form of huge tanks, heavy guns, intercontinental ballistic missiles and various other pieces of military hardware. Fighter aircraft and bombers flew in formation overhead. The spectacle went on for miles and passed directly in front of the American embassy; it appeared to be an exercise in intimidation as much as anything else. The world seems always to be preoccupied with war, either planning, fighting or contemplating when the next one will occur!

With about six months remaining in our Moscow tour, we had one more out-of-country trip to take. We had as our choice of destination either Siberia or Portugal, and we had finally settled on Portugal believing it to be a better choice for our young daughter. We flew out to London where we spent a day or two, staying in the annex of the St. James' Palace Hotel. We had just settled in when I had reason to go back down to the hotel's front desk. As I walked outside to re-enter at the main door, there was a loud explosion which temporarily staggered me. In fact, I was momentarily knocked out. Hotel security and London bobbies were quickly on the scene and the hotel entrance was sealed off. As I was revived with the help of a glass of cognac, I may have inadvertently given off some worrisome signals. Either that, or perhaps a perception that I had shifty eyes, led a bobby to confront and question me and ask me to produce my passport. When my acoster was convinced that I was legitimate and not the source of the "little homemade bomb," I was free to go. When I asked the officer why he suspected me, he said that when I registered upon our arrival, he had detected my Irish accent. It was a time when there was much tension between the British and the Irish, and any Irish accent, which I did not know I had, was always suspect in times of trouble.

We continued on our journey after that little incident, flying from Heathrow Airport in London to Faro in Portugal. At Faro, we boarded a bus and drove down to the Algarve, a beautiful stretch along the coast through orchards and orange groves. The citrus fruits in Florida used to impress us, but they paled in comparison to the oranges in Portugal. We had arrived at the ideal time of the year when the fruit was at its prime and delicious smells permeated the air. The oranges tasted as good as their aroma promised, which we soon discovered as our waiter, at the hotel dining room, would wheel his dessert cart to our table and ask for our choice of dessert – fruit or sweet? Being Newfoundlanders, we often chose both. With a sharp knife and a few quick flicks of his wrist, he would fashion a flower shape of the juiciest, tastiest orange. We didn't really need the artistry, but it was a nice touch!

Everything about the Portugal trip was enjoyable: the hotel, the food, the scenery, and the various bus trips to the many places of interest all over the Algarve. My wife and daughter rented bicycles and rode up to Prince Henry the Navigator's school of navigation situated at the southernmost tip of Europe. I stayed behind, most days, and went to the fisherman's wharf at the base of the hill where the hotel was situated. It was interesting to watch the fishermen come in with their day's catch, sometimes fish I had never seen before – octopus, large silverfish (not related to the pesky little insects that often invade living quarters), sardines that were almost as big as herring, and many other species. Every evening, hotel staff would have a fish cookout on the beach where we sampled just about everything. We had spent some time in Spain during my Canadian Air Force tour in Europe, and even though we enjoyed that country, Portugal came off as the favourite of the two. Our visit was over all too soon, and we headed back to Moscow to spend the remaining few months and to prepare for our next posting, wherever that might be.

Towards the end of the school year, news came that we would be going to New Delhi, India, following our Moscow posting. However, two months before we were to depart from Moscow, my wife's doctor in Helsinki informed her that she needed surgery. She decided it would be more convenient to have it in Ottawa than in Finland. By the time we left Moscow and returned to Ottawa where my wife spent time in hospital and underwent a month of recuperation in Ottawa's Park Lane Hotel, our New Delhi posting had been filled by someone else. All this time, I was working at External Affairs in Ottawa and, by the time we were ready to be deployed, the only available postings were to places like Islamabad, Pakistan, and to Lagos, Nigeria. Since that would necessitate our daughter going to boarding school, either in England or in Switzerland, we decided we could not take an overseas posting at that time.

PART THREE

After five years at External Affairs in Ottawa, a more exciting and profitable opportunity presented itself. My St. John's nephew, Bruce Dyke, called to ask if I would be interested in a radio operator position on the semi submersible rig, the *Sedco 709*, which was drilling for Mobil Oil off Frobisher Bay. Well, this was something I hadn't done before so, after some deliberation, I decided to accept. After spending some time in Frobisher Bay and then off the Grand Banks of Newfoundland, the rig was relocated to the North Sea. It took us approximately two weeks to make the trip across the Atlantic to Aberdeen, Scotland. We had to contend with storm-force winds and heavy seas while dealing with a less than ideal steering apparatus. The rig had two pontoons with four thrusters on each pontoon; there was no rudder and the rig was being steered by one thruster on each pontoon as we were being tossed and turned by the conditions of the ocean. We were relieved, to say the least, to arrive safely at Peterhead in Scotland, which was the maintenance area for North Sea rigs. After the rough and thoroughly unpleasant trip, we were soon given the unwelcome news that Newfoundlanders would not be permitted to work in the North Sea as it would be taking jobs from the local population. Arrangements were made to return us to Canada, to St. John's in my case. It seems odd that this fact was not known before we left Newfoundland but, as usual, the company needed a job done and, if that meant hoodwinking Newfoundlanders to get it done, then that was of little consequence...typical of the industry's behaviour towards Newfoundlanders then.

Since I was otherwise unoccupied, I thought it would be a good time to update my radio college credentials and, with this in mind, I enrolled at Red River College and headed out to Winnipeg, Manitoba. Right on cue, when I was ready to leave college and return to the workforce, my nephew Bruce called again and asked if I would be interested in a radio operator job on the *Ocean Ranger*, the biggest semi-submersible rig in the world, which was coming to drill off the Grand Banks. This rig was over 400 feet long, over 300 feet wide and 365 feet high from the pontoons to the top of the derrick. It required a dozen 5,000-pound anchors, three on each corner of the rig, to keep it in place; and it was supposed to be unsinkable. Good enough to give me confidence! So, I took the position. My family would remain in Ottawa while I would commute back and forth from St. John's. The schedule was 21 days of 12-hour shifts on the rig and 21 days at home. Later on, I would use some of my off time to remain in St. John's and, under the jurisdiction of Mobil Oil, go to the area schools to talk about the oil industry as it related to Newfoundland, and about the variety of skills students would need to acquire in order to work offshore, if they so desired. The students were eager to hear about the rig, which had been built in Japan by ODECO, and had come to

Newfoundland under the management of an American crew out of Louisiana. They wanted to know about the size of the rig and what life was like out there in the Atlantic Ocean when windstorms were raging. Many were amazed when I, referring to my log, talked about winds gusting to 91 knots, seas breaking over the front part of the rig with spray sweeping over the helideck to a height of 70 to 80 feet, and wire mesh running around the perimetre of the deck to circumvent the danger of people being blown overboard. The students, for the most part, were fascinated with all aspects of the oil industry, and with the logistics of such a gigantic rig involved in the extraction of oil from the Grand Banks. The method of travel to and from the rig, by helicopter, landing on the rig seemed to them to be quite an adventure, although many of us who had done it, sometimes in a blanket of fog, were not quite so enthusiastic. As events unfolded, some 30-plus years since I went into the schools, I wonder how these same students now feel about the safety of the rigs and the oil industry. In February 1982, the *Ocean Ranger*, the unsinkable rig, capsized and went to the bottom of the Atlantic Ocean, and the full crew of 84 men lost their lives. Then, on March 12, 2009, Cougar helicopter Flight 491 left St. John's to bring a crew of workers to their offshore jobs on the *SeaRose* production vessel and Hibernia platform, and crashed into the ocean, killing all but one of the 18 people aboard.

When the offshore oil industry began in Newfoundland, people who were sometimes without the necessary skills and experience were hired to work on the oil-drilling rigs. Other employees were just not suited for work in an offshore environment: weeks of isolation on the ocean, where incredible weather conditions were most often the scenario, played havoc with the nervous systems of certain types. Some workers arrived on the rigs already stressed from the helicopter ride out from St. John's and from the landing on the rigs in foggy and windy conditions. Such was the case when one young man came out to work, as a service hand, on the *Sedco 709*. The first time I encountered him I could sense his nervousness, but he seemed to be capable of carrying out his duties in a satisfactory manner. Like other young people, his first choice of a place of work had not been on an oil rig in the middle of the ocean. On the plus side, the pay was generous, the food and accommodations were good, and, after three weeks, he could go home for a three-week stint. Anybody could handle that, couldn't they? However, one evening, shortly after I had come on the midnight watch, I was working the ship-to-shore mobile radio system when this young man came into the radio room crying and shaking and asked me if I could please help him. Since I was copying traffic from our onshore office at the time, I told him I would be with him as soon as I could. I completed passing my traffic and went out into the gangway to look for him, and, after a little while, I found him in the galley in conversation with a man who, I later found out, was his immediate boss. I assumed that, if he still needed me, he would come back to the radio room where I returned to finish my work. I never saw him again! Things began to unravel later on, during my 12-hour shift, when no one seemed to know where the young man had gone. Then someone said that he had gone back down to his cabin, emptied his pockets saying, "I won't need this where I'm going," and disappeared somewhere in the bowels of the rig. Later he was observed kneeling with his Bible under his arm and praying. The next time he was seen was when his body was spotted floating about two miles away from the rig...a standby boat and a helicopter had gone on a search mission when I determined he was nowhere on the rig. His body was recovered and returned to the rig, where the RCMP came onboard, conducted an investigation, and took statements from a number of the crew including myself. After this, the books were closed on what was a most tragic and sad case.

Perhaps the young man might have still had health issues had he worked onshore, but at least it would have been easier for him to get the help he so obviously needed, and perhaps the loss of this young life might have been prevented. I deeply regret that I and others on the rig were unable to help him in his desperate time of need.

I was in St. John's on shore leave when the *Ocean Ranger* sank, waiting for the shift change to take place. This was a very sad event in Newfoundland history, and a great personal tragedy for those of us who worked on the rig and lost so many of our colleagues and friends. All the while I worked on the *Ocean Ranger*, I kept a log and in some entries I noted that people sometimes referred to the *Ocean Ranger* as the *Ocean Danger*, perhaps because of the many accidents that happened out there but mostly, I think, because they didn't feel it was a safe rig. In my opinion, safety issues on the *Ranger* were not a priority for management. Keeping the rig operational, at all costs, was of paramount importance. The American bosses were overbearing and often rude and ignorant, especially toward Newfoundlanders, whom I believe they considered to be their inferiors.

Rig Fever

I don't want to go down to the rig again,
To the offshore worker's life,
To the twenty-one off and the twenty-one on,
Away from my daughter and wife;

And all I ask is a good shore job
With eight hours work a day,
I'd even be willing to take a small cut
In my offshore worker's pay

I don't want to go down to the rig again
But the big bucks are hard to ignore;
I've searched all around
But I can't seem to find
A good paying job onshore
So, all I ask is for a good "Tool Push"
But the chances of that are few,
I've met quite a lot, and I know for a fact,
There's an arsehole in every crew

I must go down to the rig again,
Tho' the accident rate is high,
I'm getting well up, and I don't want to lose
An arm, a leg or an eye,
All I want is a good safety man
Who's not afraid of the bosses,
At least an RN for a medic
To, perhaps, cut back on the losses,

But I must go down to the rig again,
Cause I'm headstrong and hard to convince,
I spent eighteen months on the *Ranger*
And my friends say I should have more sense
All I want are a few more 'hitches'
And a chance at the money galore,
And then, perhaps, I'll smarten up
And finally stay on shore

– Inspired by John Masefield (1878–1967),
author of "Sea Fever," with apologies

Shortly after the *Ocean Ranger* disaster, I was offered a job with the John Shaw Corporation, the owners of the newly designed rig the *John Shaw*. This was built in Chiba, Tokyo, and was tested in Tokyo Bay. It had no rudders and was steered by manipulating its port and starboard motors. This method works fine in the calm waters of Tokyo Bay, but it was a different kettle of fish when we got out into the Mediterranean Sea, and later into the Atlantic Ocean. I had decided not to go to Japan to join the *John Shaw* at the start of its journey to Newfoundland, but I did agree to join the rig in Egypt, so I flew out to Cairo and, 24 hours later, boarded the rig in Port Said. It is no exaggeration to say that the rig barely squeezed through the Suez Canal. As we passed through, it was interesting to view the Sinai Desert and, again, to witness evidence of yet another battle – wrecked tanks and guns, remnants of the 1967 war between Egypt and Israel. We arrived at the eastern end of the Mediterranean Sea and passed Malta on our starboard bow and Tunisia on our port side. Shortly after, we ran into a vicious storm which, according to later radio reports, wrecked a number of smaller vessels sailing behind us.

As we travelled onward, we anchored overnight in Gibraltar Bay. I got the thrill of my life when I awoke the next morning, went up on deck, saw the famous Rock of Gibraltar, and recalled its historic significance. We refueled in Gibraltar, took on supplies and, because of the many complaints regarding the steering problems in rough waters, we were offered the option of leaving the rig and being flown home. A few people took the option, but most of us continued on westward to battle the Atlantic. I had occasion to wish I had chosen to fly before we arrived safely home.

The 1942 Atlantic crossing to participate in World War II had been dangerous enough and I wished, during the *John Shaw*'s crossing, that I had never undertaken this second perilous journey; a wartime trek was one thing, but to put my existence at risk in such a treacherous peacetime adventure was certainly foolhardy. The 36 days that it took for the *John Shaw* to go from the Suez Canal to Halifax, Nova Scotia, were among the most stressful days of my life. It seems to me that all safety precautions had been abandoned in an attempt to cross the 50 degree longitude W as quickly as possible; I believe this was due to some financial issues in the form of extra fees, etc. The rig was being towed by an ocean-going tug and was making very little headway, sometimes as little as one or two knots because of the strong ocean currents and the resistance that was being produced by the submerged pontoons. We were being buffeted by huge swells and seas to the extent that the rig was constantly in danger of becoming a derelict. In order to increase our speed and cross over the all-important 50 degree longitude W, the decision was made to deballast the rig. Once the pontoons were raised to ocean level, we certainly moved much faster, but our stability was also greatly affected so that we were being tossed around like a cork. In addition to these devastating conditions, the bearings around the propeller shaft were constantly overheating and two seamen were assigned to keep a continuous stream of cold water flowing over it. The overall situation was so dire that a helicopter, with Japanese engineers, was sent out from Halifax to observe the rig's progress and to offer whatever assistance they could, if needed. However the worst of the trip was already over by then as we were in calmer waters.

In addition to the strain of the travel conditions, our rig super-intendent, who shall remain nameless, was one of the most despicable human beings I have ever known.

Once we were situated on the Grand Banks, we encountered the usual storms. The *John Shaw*, being a new rig, had sensors all around the exterior that were capable of measuring the currents, wind speed, wave height, etc., not that it made us feel any safer to know that winds were clocked in at 91 knots in the gusting, and to observe the barograph going off the scale! The standard procedure on the *John Shaw* was for the evacuation of all non-essential personnel if there was any prediction of storm-force winds blowing up from the East Coast of the United States. One particular storm printout showed 81-foot seas hitting the rig; this resulted in some structural damage, and provided some tense hours for those essential persons who remained on board, namely the captain, the chief engineer, the ballast control operator and the radio operator – me. This was one of the worst storms I experienced during my six years working on the rigs on the Grand Banks, the foggiest and most dangerous place in the world for offshore oil exploration. Sometimes, I think I felt safer in Normandy during the war; at least then, if I heard a shell coming, I could find refuge in my dugout. There was no such sanctuary in a vicious storm on an oil rig offshore. I was finally coming to the conclusion that I had had enough of white-knuckle helicopter flights travelling to and from the rig, the commercial travel, the anxiety of being away from my family, and the jeopardy of working on oil rigs. I gave my notice, worked my final 21-day shift and headed back home to retirement; after all I was now 62, and there couldn't be anything more interesting than that in my future, could there?

While I was still serving with the Royal Canadian Air Force, I had heard about an outfit called WUSC, World University Services of Canada, based in Ottawa. At that time, I talked with Dr. John Watson, who headed up the operation, and got some information about their countries of engagement, the types of positions available, and the qualifications necessary to work overseas. Later, after resigning my position on the *John Shaw*, I was sitting in my living room one evening watching a documentary about the famine and drought conditions in Sudan and Ethiopia, and I immediately recognized a representative from WUSC who was talking about their involvement in the aid program there. Just out of curiosity and, as my wife says, because I am something of a telephone addict, I called. Lo and behold, Watson was still with the organization. He told me about a few available positions in Sudan, one of which was for a communications manager. Upon learning about my qualifications and experience, he offered me the latter position, and asked if I would present myself for processing as soon as possible. When my wife returned home, she looked at me and said, "Why the Cheshire Cat grin, what have you committed to now?"

When I asked her how she'd like to go to Africa, she just gave me a "look" and went on about her business. However, when I went to Khartoum, the capital of Sudan, in October, Ruby followed me three months later.

Africa's weather, when I arrived there, was nothing like the pleasant fall conditions I had left behind in Ottawa. However, I would become accustomed, over the next couple of years, to the extreme heat, the lack of moisture in the air, the scarcity of precipitation and, a little more difficult to tolerate, the *haboobs* (sand storms) of Africa.

I arrived at the Khartoum airport just after midnight, after flying out from London, England, and was met by the head of the transport operation, Rudy Rodriguez. The usually over-crowded streets were empty as there was an 11:00 p.m. curfew in effect. We were able to proceed to the Sahara Hotel where I was billeted until my wife arrived. We then moved into a very nice house which was owned, and had previously been occupied, by the CEO of the French company Total. It was a large stone home surrounded by an eight-foot, well-lit stone wall with a security gate that was always kept locked. Servants' quarters were attached to the house, and a separate area was provided for the guard/gardener, Mohammed, who chose to sleep on a cot on the porch with his trusty machete by his side. We were truly thankful that our house and car were air-conditioned, and also that we could access the roof by stairs in the foyer. That was a pleasant place to sit, underneath the gigantic eucalyptus tree, providing we went up there before 7:00 a.m. as after that it was too hot. I remember telling my wife to drink her tea quickly before it, the tea, got too hot! In the early evenings, we'd sometimes go up to see the flocks of beautiful birds that would come to roost in the trees, and also to get a little exercise by taking a brisk walk around the perimeter.

When we sat upon the roof in the early morning, we felt like we were living in Bible times. There was a cacophony of sounds as snorting camels mingled with the drone of many Arabic dialects as the population began the difficult task of eking out yet another day of living. The roads were crowded with local men in their *jalabiyas*, riding on donkeys laden down with pots and pans, and with some foods like mangoes, juice and milk for sale or trade, all enveloped in clouds of sand and dust.

Speaking of the roof reminds me of the location of our water tank in that area. Before taking a bath, we would have to fill the tub and wait quite some time before the water cooled to bath temperature. Looking out over one section of the roof, we could see women and children, naked or dressed in rags, emerging from shacks which had been thrown together using pieces of cardboard, twigs, rags, bits of metal and whatever they could scrape together to provide some sort of shelter from the scorching sun. Miserable little fires would be started and some sort of food would be prepared. It was heartbreaking to see so much poverty and need, and it made us feel extremely guilty to be living in relative luxury in the midst of it all. We were able to do some little good over the next couple of years but it was something like putting a Band-Aid on a tsunami.

In accordance with an unwritten policy, we were expected to hire Sudanese as household staff. Thus, we acquired the services of a chauffeur, a cook, a maid, a general helper and our guard/gardener, Mohammed. The salaries we paid them were modest according to our standard but, to them, it was a small fortune. In addition, they had a safe, comfortable place to live and plenty of food to eat. Our cook, Almaz, prepared such huge amounts of food that we soon realized she was feeding many more people than us and our household staff. With the help of Mohammed, she was sneaking in not only some of her family and friends but also those of Mohammed, when we were absent or were otherwise occupied. We had to deal with the dishonesty aspect, and we put some restrictions on the number of extra people she could supply but, for the most part, we didn't mind helping feed a few people who would have gone hungry otherwise.

The servants were good workers who kept everything spotlessly clean, and the house lizards under control. My wife used to get a little unnerved if they were running up the walls or running out from underneath the furniture. For the first time in my life, I also got a service I didn't really need, as Teflon, our general maid, ironed every piece of clothing I owned including my socks and underwear. (My wife, not unexpectedly, didn't continue the practice after we left Africa.) Mohammed was an adept gardener and kept everything looking beautiful. In the evenings, he would make the rounds, closing the wooden window shutters, lighting all the lamps around the wall and those scattered strategically around the garden, and we'd settle in for the night – lucky thing we had lots of good reading material and music! Sometimes the power would go out and there would be total blackness until Mohammed started up the generator. This he always did promptly unless it happened to be on a Thursday, which was servants' day off, when he inevitably returned home inebriated and had difficulty in even finding the generator. He did manage, however, to keep track of his live chicken, which he brought home, tucked under his arm, on Thursday evenings for beheading and for cooking the next day. He cooked over a charcoal fire in his living area where he also kept a stone jar and a ladle attached to the branch of a tree; this was to keep his drinking water cool and it was a very effective method. Mohammed always managed to look dignified; he was always well-groomed and proved himself to be a loyal servant, in spite of his getting plastered every Thursday. He was entitled to extend his Thursdays off to include nights but, if I were in some other part of the country, as I often was, he would never leave my wife alone on the premises. He inevitably turned up, intoxicated, with his chicken, did his chores and, with his machete in place, proceeded to sleep off his binge.

Upon presenting myself, the morning after my arrival, to Alan Pratley, head of the World Food Program under the United Nations, I knew why a communications manager was so urgently needed. The system, such as it was, was in utter chaos. A meeting with the NGOs (nongovernmental organization) – 105 members – was arranged to discuss the situation as it pertained to the central, eastern, western and southern regions of Sudan. I also met my technical advisor and interpreter, Maj. Khalid Abdullah Al Taher, not only a highly skilled technician but also a man of fine character and integrity. Khalid had fought in the Six-Day War against Israel on the side of Egypt and had since returned to Sudan to serve his home country. He set up a meeting with the Sudanese Minister of Communications to make our request for the necessary supplies of crystals, passes and permits. The Motorola radio equipment, about half million dollars worth of it, had already been shipped from Chicago prior to my arrival, and would arrive in Khartoum soon after. The Sudanese minister, being one of many of the country's corrupt officials, asserted there would be no business transacted before he received an agreed-upon supply of scotch, the preferred drink for the (non-drinking) Muslims. I have no knowledge of what occurred behind the scenes, as I had no part in the negotiations, but, eventually, all requests were honoured.

Khalid and his team began erecting antennas throughout the Western area, El Fasher, the capital of North Darfur, El Geneina, Juba in the southern area, and Port St. John of the eastern area and, finally, Khartoum. When everything was in place, and we had hired a number of English-speaking Sudanese radio/teletype operators, traffic started to flow immediately and efficiently.

It seems that many of the Sudanese officials, in spite of all the aid they were receiving from the Western world, resented our presence in their country, and revelled in putting as many obstacles as possible in our path. For instance, no sooner was the communications system up and running when Sudanese Brigadier Abraham Albino started insisting that I fire all the English-speaking operators from southern Sudan and replace them with Arabic-speaking employees of his choice. This would have created an impossible working environment, and so I refused and passed the problem along to Rodriguez. He solved it with a compromise to hire an equal number, between 30 and 40 people, of the Brigadier's choice. They didn't do any communications work, but they received equivalent pay for doing odd chores or, in most cases, for doing nothing at all except to unroll their prayer mats and pray to Allah five times a day.

While in Sudan, I had a small plane, a five-passenger Cessna, and a pilot to transport me to all regions under the jurisdiction of the World Food Program. Khalid and I periodically made inspections and took troubleshooting trips to several places, but mostly we went to El Fasher, Port St. John and Juba. Juba was something of a difficult spot, and going there often posed a security risk for us. There was considerable friction between the rebels, under the command of Colonel John Garang of the Sudanese People's Liberation Army, and the corrupt Sudanese government. Another faction was the Christian element of southern Sudan, which suffered terrible atrocities under the Sudanese army. Corruption was so rampant, not only in Juba

but in the surrounding areas of Wau and Yei, that most
commerce ceased to exist, and it was a constant struggle for
locals to overcome the many obstacles of daily living. Farms
and homes were destroyed and people, if they managed to avoid
being killed, fled and hid out in other parts of the country.
Many women and children were kidnapped, raped and
murdered during the almost nightly raids, and it was hard to
determine who was responsible, the Sudanese Army or the
rebels. I remember one of my radio operators coming into
my office one day and asking for three days off so that he
could grieve; he had just received word that his family had
all been slain, and their farm and animals confiscated by the
government.

It was necessary, on one of our trips to Juba, to travel on a
Boeing 707 which was carrying relief supplies to southern
Sudan, including Juba. A problem presented itself in that the
rebels had a SAM-6 site (Service to Air Missile Site) quite close
to the airport. It had the capability to shoot down aircraft
flying at an altitude not exceeding 13,000 feet. Consequently,
we flew in above that, at around 14,000 feet, and approached
the opposite end of the runway maintaining a circular pattern.
We landed without incident; the plane was unloaded, Khalid
and I attended to our business, and we departed Juba, the
plane climbing as quickly and as high as it could, this being
significantly easier to do now that the plane was so much lighter
in weight. Juba was not one of our favourite places to go, and
we were always greatly relieved to get out of there safely.

Looking at El Fasher, and the whole of the Darfur region of
Africa today, via television, it's hard to recognize it as the El
Fasher I knew in the 1980s. During my time there, the World

Food Program maintained a station and, apart from a mosque, a bevy of squalid mud huts, and a smattering of people, there was little else. Flying in and over the desert from Khartoum though, and coming in over El Fasher, was a rather pleasant experience because, suddenly, there was a little vegetation which included several varieties of flowering plants and shrubs. There was even a pool about 100 feet long which, unfortunately, was usually filled with stagnant green water. Flying over the desert, there were lots of sand dunes and, occasionally, we'd see nomadic tribes with their camels resting in these areas and sheltering under the date palm. While we had to land on a narrow strip, barely capable of handling our small plane, today there are landing strips built by the Russians and Chinese, to handle their fighter jets. The whole area has been inundated with thousands of refugees fleeing persecution and terrorism from many parts of Africa. Aid workers and other entities are attempting to deal with the devastation of hunger, famine and disease that is rampant throughout Darfur.

While we were in Khartoum, there were approximately 400,000 refugees – 20,000 of them children – and this made up about half the city's total population. When stopping at a traffic light in the city, swarms of children would emerge from God only knows where, and they would cover the car like flies on molasses. It was impossible to give handouts to so many, and it was mindboggling and heartrending to know that there were so many hungry, homeless children in the city and that, in spite of the tremendous efforts being made by the United Nations World Food Program, Mercy Corps, World Vision, Band Aid, UNICEF and many others, there was so much more that needed to be done. Enormous quantities of food were being brought into the country, but with so much corruption going on, and the prob-lems associated with tribal hatred and conflict, and the lack of trained transport drivers, much of it was not getting to where it was supposed to go.

At the time, there were between 200 and 300 transport trucks – Volvo and Fiat models which had been donated by Sweden and Italy – awaiting drivers. Training was taking place, but even when the trucks were ready to roll and drivers were prepared, it was imperative to place a driver and a relief driver, who were from the same tribe, into each truck. This took some doing. Sometimes, the drivers would profess to be from the same tribe in order to get jobs, but when they got out on the road, there was often hell to pay when such was not the case. At least now the food was starting to move. There had been hundreds of tons of food, some of which was being stored in warehouses and hangars, but much of it was sitting out in the open where it was being stolen, eaten by dogs and other animals, or being destroyed by the heat and sand storms.

The trucks were finally loaded, and the drivers headed for the distribution points of El Obeid, Costa, Nyala and El Fasher. Theirs wasn't an enviable job; they were pointed in the right direction, and they followed the hard-packed sandy paths across the desert. The main camel trail ran from Cairo, Egypt, down through Sudan, and everything that moved on the desert was at the mercy of camel rustlers, common thieves, murderers, deserters, thugs and riffraff from the various tribes of the surrounding countries.

At this time, Colonel John Garang, Leader of the SPLA, was living in exile in Addis Ababa, the capital of Ethiopia, and he was inciting violent action by his followers in Sudan. Every day at three o'clock, he did a radio broadcast, beamed towards Sudan, to the effect that anything that moved over the Sudanese Desert or on the Nile River would be ambushed, and any aircraft flying in the vicinity would be shot down. Of course, this was merely a wild outrageous threat, which he had no way of implementing, but it served his purpose of maintaining control over his band of hoodlums. In spite of his threats, in excess of 800,000 tons of food was transported over the desert and on the river.

The rustlers, and others of the criminal element, were well aware of the food-laden trucks and often lay in wait for them. At the very beginning of the food delivery operation in Sudan, 12 trucks that had gone out were ambushed, all the food taken, and the 24 drivers brutally murdered. Finally, they were given some protection as the relief driver of each track was armed with an AK-47.

Occasionally, it rained in Africa and, when that happened, the *wadis* (the dry river beds) often proved to be a big obstacle to transportation as they filled up with water. However, over time, this problem was corrected by the construction of the Irish bridges; these were merely concrete slabs poured in the *wadis* before the rains began.

Even though some of the actual transport problems had been solved, there were still many other issues to be addressed. Often, drivers helped themselves to some of the contents of the trucks, or else they made detours to their villages and unloaded food for their families and friends. The leaders of each village, upon receiving a shipment, skimmed some off the top, particularly cooking oil, and much of the stolen food would later appear on the black market to be sold at exorbitant prices. Before the communications system was installed, there had been no way of keeping track of the transport vehicles, to know whether or not they had reached their destination, or how much of the shipment they were still carrying if and when they did arrive. With the communications system operational, all aspects of food distribution improved considerably, and consequently, the necessity to physically travel to a number of trouble spots was reduced.

In Khartoum, the British operated an upscale club complete with a library, swimming pool, garden restaurant, and several other amenities. After World War II, the British and Egyptians were the administrators of Sudan, and this club had been used by the officers of each country. According to a member of the staff (a female librarian who had been there during that time) it had been a place of pomp and ceremony, and of incredible luxury, with seven red Rolls-Royces on the property, for example. Some of the land surrounding that area, which had been lavishly land-scaped and cared for, had been reclaimed by the continuous wind and sand slowly but surely moving eastward toward the Nile. But the club and its surrounding area was still a beautiful spot in the mid-1980s.

The British graciously opened up the Sudan Club to Canadians, Australians, and people of a few other nationalities that were in the city. As was the practice of the British in colonial times, they took advantage of the local population and always had a full complement of servants. Club members could swim at any hour of the day or night, engage in a variety of sports, take advantage of the well-stocked library, or just sit at tables under the trees or umbrellas while waiters hovered around refilling tea and coffee cups or bringing soft drinks...no alcohol however. At meal times, there was always a good supply of various foods: lots of curry, for sure, and all at a very reasonable price. It was undeniably enjoyable, especially on an unbearably hot day, which was every day actually, to be able to take advantage of the pool and the other amenities but, once one exited the club, an entirely different world was there. There was no way to justify the privileges experienced by a few compared with the utter want experienced by so many others.

My daughter, who was studying in England at the time, came out to visit us in Sudan, and she was sickened, as were we, to see swarms of hungry, sometimes naked kids raiding the garbage bins outside the Sudan Club while Sudanese policemen, with heavy whips, chased them away. What we had discarded would have been a feast for them, and they couldn't even have that! One day we observed a stark-naked boy, probably 13 or 14, staggering blindly past the Sudan Club wall, nothing more than a walking skeleton, completely oblivious to his surroundings...an image that I shall never forget. My daughter went to the Red Sea on a scuba diving expedition and, on her way back to Khartoum, she spent some time in Kassala at a refugee camp operated by a Dutch couple. She was deeply influenced by all that she saw there, and she partially credits the whole African experience for her decision to make human services her life's work.

Another club in Khartoum was the Sahara Club, which was frequented primarily by commercial people doing business in the capital. It wasn't considered to be as secure a facility as the Sudan Club. One Sunday night, a bomb exploded there and several people were killed. The explosion was attributed, by some, to al-Qaeda; this was never proven to be so, but Osama bin Laden was said to be a resident of Khartoum at that time.

As in most foreign countries, Americans have their own clubs and such was the case in Khartoum, but the only times we went there was when we had a yearning for a good hamburger.

One of the ever-present sounds in Sudan was the droning of the Muslim call to prayer, five times a day. The dedication of the Muslims to Allah was evident everywhere, especially in the marketplaces. A brisk business would be in progress and, when the call to prayer sounded, the curtains would be pulled down over the individual stalls, prayer mats would be unrolled and the worshipers would kneel, facing Mecca, and perform their prayer rituals. Those of us professing to be Christians, infidels to them, were obviously annoying to some of the most radical belivers. As far as I know, there were only two Christian churches in Khartoum, an Anglican church and the Baptist church we attended. At one point, one of the extremist factions showed their disdain for us by placing a dead donkey at the entrance to the Baptist church where we gathered on Sunday nights. This was an open-sided, thatched-roof building, and the sound of our singing carried quite a distance over the still night air. It was determined that the donkey had been killed elsewhere and dragged to the church porch, so we would be sure to see it when we exited the building. We could not presume to have equal rights to worship in a Muslim country, and we knew we could expect a certain amount of harassment.

One of the most weird and scary experiences I had in Sudan was when I agreed to go with Khalid to the wedding of his niece. The ceremony was held in the countryside and was a huge celebration by Sudanese standards. Since I was the guest of honour, I was ensconced in a regal-sized chair, draped in white silk, in the centre of a huge tent, which had been erected for the occasion. The floor of the tent was covered with flamboyant Arabian carpets. All around the perimeter of the tent were banks of speakers emitting high-pitched, mesmerizing Sudanese music. Women performed tribal dances for our entertainment; although they were not as wild or frenetic as a number of Dervish dancers, they seemed to be demon-possessed and were frightening to watch. The refreshments offered, both food and drink, did not look too enticing either but, so as not to offend my host, I gingerly sampled a little of everything offered to me. While all this was going on, Khalid seemed to have disappeared, and as I turned to try to locate him, I was shocked to see six or seven Sudanese Army soldiers standing directly behind me, holding AK-47s and bull whips. Had Khalid tricked me into some kind of compromising situation? I was scared out of my wits and I wondered what in the hell was going on. Khalid appeared soon after and said that he had been close by all the time, and he had noticed my uneasiness. He informed me that the soldiers were there not to harm me, but for my protection; he didn't say from whom. He also affirmed that the soldiers were what they called "bad Muslims" and were probably associated with bin Laden. I was anxious to summon my driver to get me out of there, but Khalid urged me to stay a little longer, to save face, and he would personally guarantee my safety. The conclusion of that evening was a great relief to me, to say the least.

There was adequate spare time in Khartoum for me to be a part of a band we formed and called Sweet Charity, and which we used to raise money for a variety of worthy causes. Our WUSC business manager, George, was an excellent guitarist, a fine showman and singer. Another amazing guitarist, from England, joined our group as did a couple of singers, nurses from a group called Gold. A young technician, Keith, from St. John's, who was our all-purpose man, and I, the drummer, completed the group. We provided good music, became quite popular and were in much demand.

Of all the interesting things we did while we were in Africa, one of the best was an all-day trip we took on the Nile River. The lush vegetation along the river's banks was in direct contrast to the vast expanse of sand of the Sahara Desert, which, unfortunately, has been slowly but surely moving ever closer to what little vegetation still remains in Sudan. We saw evidence of this occurring as we flew over what had been living areas but were now covered by the ever-encroaching sands. As our tour boat meandered down the river, large tree branches with beehive shaped nests waved overhead; these beautiful nests were the homes of wild canaries. The many varieties of birds, and their magnificent colours, were a joy to behold, not only on the Nile, but throughout Africa. Further down the river, we came to the adobe brickmaking area where dozens of workers wheeled barrows filled with the deep red-coloured earth to large smouldering fire pits where the process of heating and shaping the mudbricks was taking place. Mud huts were everywhere all along the riverbank, and swarms of young, naked, or scantily clad youngsters were running around and seemingly enjoying their lives immensely.

We observed lots of bullrushes along the shoreline, but we were unable to pinpoint the exact location where the Pharaoh's daughter plucked baby Moses and his basket out of the river to take him to live in the royal household. We stopped looking when we remembered that that event had taken place on the Egyptian part of the Nile, not in Sudan. All in all, we had an enjoyable day on the river. They even sold us bottles of Coca-Cola, which was restricted at the Sudan Club because the Muslims believed that Coca-Cola was owned and operated by Israel. They offered Pepsi Cola instead. Go figure!

When I first flew out from Khartoum to El Fasher, our pilot Tim (I never learned his surname) pointed out a gigantic volcano crater in a rock complex known as Jebel Marra (Arabic for "bad mountains"). Tim offered to give me a tour and, before I could agree or disagree, he was already inside the crater and flying a tight circle around its interior. At the bottom, there was a large accumulation of what I was told was salt but more likely was ash. I was so impressed with this little sojourn that I mentioned it to my wife and daughter and, later on, Tim gave them the same tour. They commented on the fact that Tim seemed to use the automatic pilot a lot while flying over the desert, and often dozed off en route. It was, understandably, a monotonous trip for him but still a rather dangerous practice because, as I told my daughter, he didn't actually have the benefit of automatic pilot.

I must make mention of a rather amusing little incident that happened at a shop in Khartoum where I had my driver, Reddy, take me to buy a safari suit. Reddy went in to scout out the place and came back out, waving his arms and saying "No! No, Mr. Frank! Don't go in!" Now my curiosity was aroused so in I went, Reddy following close behind. Several scowling Sudanese men, with a Palestinian Liberation Organization (PLO) flag on the wall behind them, just glared at me as I inquired about their ability to speak English. One of them finally said, "What country you come from?" When I replied that I was from Canada, their faces lit up, and the spokesman said, "Come in, my friend, have some tea. I have cousin in Toronto, uncle in Montréal. You must forgive us, we thought you American." The reason Reddy had not wanted me to go into this particular outlet was, as soon as he entered, he recognized it as the place where an employee of the American embassy had been killed a few months earlier.

Reddy was very concerned about my welfare and he was always trying to do things that pleased me. Of course being a refugee from Ethiopia, he was dependent on me for his job and this could have motivated him. When my wife and I first moved into our house, he appeared with two skinny loaves of bread under his arm, no wrapping, but with a wide smile on his face. He also had a few lemons, two mangoes, some tiny African bananas and a few tomatoes. When we broke open the bread that Reddy was so proud of, it was full of boll weevils. The Irish nurses laughed at us when we said we couldn't eat the bread because it was full of bugs; they told us to get over it and not to be such wimps; the bugs were a good source of protein, and hadn't hurt them any.

Reddy also took us to a store which he said was a special spot for foreigners, but all we could find there that was familiar to us were canned peaches, canned beans and canned tomatoes. For a while, all we ate was beans over rice, tomatoes over rice, and peaches, mangoes or bananas for dessert. After a couple of weeks, we were granted permission to shop at the well-stocked British store where everything we desired was available to us. Reddy was happy with this new arrangement as we were able to keep him supplied with milk for his children, plus a lot of other goodies.

I arrived at my office one morning to find a distinguished-looking gentleman waiting for me. He turned out to be Dr. Ted Hurd, a former moderator of the United Church of Canada. He was overseeing a Serving in Mission (SIM) agricultural project in southern Sudan. He was having trouble with his communications equipment and was in need of my assistance. The farm was 50 or 60 miles away from Khartoum over very rough desert roads with only a few ill-defined markers to track the route. However, Ted assured me that he had made the trip several times before and, with the help of his own tracking system and a little common sense, he had not experienced any difficulties. The only real concern was that the expected rains would begin before we could reach our destination.

So, we proceeded on our merry way, without incident, until the dreaded precipitation did start. It began as a kind of drizzle. After taking a bathroom break at a camp area where, incidentally, Ted seemed to know everybody, we continued toward the farm. All the while the rain was increasing in intensity until it seemed as if the heavens had suddenly opened up and was intent upon drowning us. I had never before experienced such a severe storm. The torrential rain, the claps of deafening thunder, and the continuous bolts of lightning bombarding the desert were frightening. All the while, the sandy desert was getting muddier and muddier, slowing our progress until we were becoming quite concerned. Suddenly, Ted said, "We are okay Frank, there's the farm straight ahead." Almost at the same time, the station wagon came to an abrupt stop totally mired in mud, almost like quicksand. In spite of all of Ted's efforts, it was impossible to move.

Ted, a most resourceful and competent man, probably in his 60s at the time, was used to dealing with all kinds of emergency situations in that part of the world, and he decided there was only one source of action to take. "I guess I'll just have to take a walk, Frank," and he rolled up his pant legs and with his flashlight in hand, stepped out into the mire, and God only knows what other dangers. He told me to stay put as there was absolutely nothing I could do to help. So I sat and enjoyed the show that Mother Nature was presenting.

Just minutes after Ted had started off on his journey, the vehicle began a violent rocking motion. My heart started pounding as I had no idea what was happening. Then, during a brilliant lightning flash, I could see a number of African men with the rain glistening on their faces. I didn't know if they were attempting to free the vehicle or planning to kill me. If the latter were the case, I decided to go out fighting, and so I locked the doors, picked up a tire iron from underneath the seat... little good that would have done since I was greatly out-numbered, but I was scared to death and had to do something, however insignificant. Fortunately, before I needed to take action, I saw a single light approaching, followed by the two headlights of some sort of farm vehicle, and I knew that Ted had arrived safely at the farm and had sent help. The men outside the station wagon quickly disappeared and, eventually, the vehicle was released from its muddy trap and towed to the farm.

Several Canadians from Saskatchewan were there awaiting my arrival. Some scorpions who had come in out of the storm, two or three of them, had also found their way into our accommodations. This was unusual as the farm was well pro-tected against those sometimes dangerous and deadly invaders, but someone, in their haste to get shelter from the storm, had neglected to put the scorpion net where it was supposed to be, underneath the door. This problem was remedied by the experts, and we all sat down to a sumptuous meal. Before going to bed I had to make sure there were no unwelcome intruders there; I stripped the bed and, after wrapping myself securely and getting my mosquito net in place, I laid down to rest and to recuperate from my journey thus far. After a peaceful night, I investigated Ted's problem, found it to be a minor one – a glitch in the radio telegraph system, RTTY, which was easily remedied by replacing a vital part and installing a new ground wire. With everyone happy, we headed back to Khartoum over a different and dryer route.

Back in Khartoum, routine work continued until something very unexpected and frightening occurred. On April 15, 1986, word came that the United States, under President Ronald Reagan, had bombed Tripoli, the capital of Libya. This was particularly alarming for us because WUSC House, where most of the Canadian personnel lived, and our house were in very close proximity, just across the street actually, from the Libyan Embassy in Khartoum. This always seemed threatening to us even before the United States attacked Libya. Shortly after the news came, one Sunday night while Reddy, our driver, waited at the gate to drive us to church, our area warden arrived and ordered us to remain inside our house. Our guard, Mohammed, locked the gates, closed up the wooden window shutters, and barricaded the front, back and roof doors. We felt completely isolated but relatively safe while we awaited further orders.

It was still necessary for me to go to work on Monday morning and when Reddy came to drive me, he told me there were tanks in the streets and an army of Sudanese soldiers, or at least there were individuals dressed like Sudanese soldiers. Knowing what we did about the Sudanese Army, we knew they were just spoiling for a fight and it would not take much to provoke them. Occasionally, we would hear gunfire, whether from the Sudanese or from the Libyans, we had no idea. However, there were no reported injuries or deaths from this. During the course of the next day or two, while I was being escorted to work, there was much activity at WUSC House. Americans were being accosted in the streets and threatened and, as a result, several Americans had gone to WUSC House to request Canadian flags and emblems that they could attach to their clothing or to their backpacks. It was considered safer to be recognized as a Canadian rather than as an American in this scary and volatile environment. It very soon became apparent that the situation was becoming so dangerous that evacuation of nonessential personnel was imminent. On the third or fourth day after the attack, I arrived home and told my wife to throw a few things together in preparation for evacuation to Nairobi, Kenya. I was to remain behind because of my involvement with communications. Before she was able to proceed to the assembly point, however, the word came that there had been a change in plans and that all personnel were to be evacuated. Consequently, we were picked up and taken to an area where the US Marines were in charge. Our passports were collected and the necessary documentation prepared. When everything was in order and a convoy was formed, we were ready to be escorted to another destination.

The string of buses, jeeps and half-tracks was led by armed Marines on motorcycles and, after two remaining vehicles from other collection points joined the procession, armed guards took their positions at the rear. Each vehicle carried an armed Marine, and armed outriders flanked each side of the vehicles. Our destination, we soon learned, was the American Embassy where we were welcomed and royally entertained at the Ambassador's residence. After several hours, without any information as to our next move, and when it was pitch black with that total darkness of African nights, we were assigned to our buses. There were only enough Canadians to fill one but, with the large number of Americans being evacuated, there were perhaps eight to ten different means of transport lined up on the embassy grounds. Our convoy was led by the Ambassador in his long black limousine, with US flags flying, and interspersed with an entourage of armed military trucks and motorcycle Marines. With lights flashing and sirens blaring, we rode to the airport, where a Swiss Airbus was waiting to fly us to Nairobi. It was like a scene from a James Bond movie, and must have been a most impressive sight to anyone watching. Bin Laden, if in Khartoum as rumoured, may have been with some of his followers among the crowds on the street leading to the airport. However, no one fired on us and we arrived safely. We were not taken to the terminal but to the outer end of the tarmac where the Airbus was waiting. We waited while a final security check of the plane was being conducted. Finally, we were able to board and be seated. There was a collective sigh of relief that this part of the ordeal was over and we were unharmed.

Once we were on the ground in Nairobi the passports were re-turned to their rightful owners, but things did not run smoothly for me nor for an American female passenger who had been evacuated with her infant daughter. Our passports were missing! How this could have happened, between the Marine collection point and our arrival in Nairobi, remains a mystery.

We assumed that the documents had somehow been acciden-tally separated from the pile, and that they would be forwarded to us when the error became evident. However, this did not happen and, to my knowledge, the passports were never recovered. I wonder who might have used them and for what purpose? In the meantime, the passport-carrying passengers, including my wife, were being transported to the Hilton Hotel where a huge reception had been prepared. But my fellow passenger, her daughter and I were held on the plane. Eventually after several hours had passed, and advocates from the American Embassy and an agent from the Canadian high commission appeared on the scene, negotiations took place with the Kenyan officials and, around 4:00 a.m., we were taken to the hotel to rejoin our group.

I have almost always known the Americans to be generous and friendly toward their fellow man, and such was the case throughout the evacuation process and our arrival in Kenya. We Canadians were treated exactly the same as were their own people. We were assigned our individual rooms, fed delicious meals, all free of charge, and we were treated with the utmost courtesy. A direct line to the US was established and, to our surprise and thankfulness, a line to Canada. At that time, our daughter was attending college in the States and, since she was our main concern for contact, we were able to talk to her almost immediately. Everyone was given a limit of five minutes each at first, then, after they had made their most important calls, the lines were available at all hours for whatever time needed for the next 48 hours, and of course, all calls were free of charge.

We were able to see the sights of Nairobi during the next few days (some of which were disturbing and heartbreaking, especially the degree of leprosy still prevalent in this part of Kenya). Not knowing how long we would be there, nor if we would be returning to Sudan or going back to Canada, we were becoming a little restless. An American doctor, who had been in charge of Mercy Corps in Sudan, decided that he and his wife would arrange some distractions for themselves and for us. One of the most enjoyable was a Safari.

Two Land Rovers, with mostly Americans on board, headed out, and we had a day of unique experiences. Although the only lion we saw was a dead one, we did see a variety of other African animals in their natural habitat: giraffes, hippos, rhinos, monkeys, wildebeest and others. We also observed some interesting horticultural species. Our guide pointed out thorn bushes which bore the largest spikes imaginable... nothing like the "stinging nettles" of Newfoundland. We wondered if they were the same kind of thorns referred to in the Bible, describing the crucifixion of Jesus, when a crown of thorns was placed on his head as a means of mockery. If so, the pain of such barbs being pushed into the skin had to be excruciating.

When we returned to our hotel, word had arrived that we would not be leaving Nairobi for at least another week to ten days as no decision had been made about whether or not we would be returning to Sudan. We then resolved to take a trip on the Kenyan railway and travel down to Mombasa, on the Indian Ocean. We boarded the train in the late evening, went to the dining room for dinner, and settled down for the night. In the early morning we were awakened by the train steward playing a tune on a miniature xylophone, a traditional custom on this route of the railway; I understand it was his way of announcing the serving of breakfast in the dining car. He also informed us that we were travelling through Kenya's National Park and, if we were interested, we would be treated to a most wonderful sight, that of a vast expanse of open country where a multitude of animals roamed. All we had to do was look out the window as we proceeded through the park.

We saw gazelles frolicking quite close to the train, wildebeest, elephants, zebras and many other species native to Africa. To see such a variety of animals up close in their natural habitat was indeed a thrill and a spectacle we will always remember. We had travelled by train from Ottawa to Vancouver and had thoroughly enjoyed that trip, but this Kenyan journey surpassed any other train trip including the one we had taken from Moscow to Rovaniemi on the Arctic Circle. It even surpassed our Newfoundland "Bullet" train trips of many years ago.

We arrived in Mombasa where the porter from our hotel ushered us into vehicles and drove us to the White Sands Hotel on the sandy beaches of the Indian Ocean. The accommodations, food and entertainment all measured up to our expectations. We slept under mosquito nets, and we always remembered to take our quinine tablets to protect us from malaria. We met people at the resort from South Africa, England, Australia and other parts of the world.

I remember stepping out of the villa to take walks on the beach in the relative cool of the evenings and could not believe the number of strange looking creatures that were coming up out of the sand, some of them extremely ugly. My wife hurried back inside at the sight of something that looked like a large tailless rat. We used to sit on the beach in the daytime when it was not too hot and, although many people swam in the warm waters of the ocean, it didn't look too clean to us and we never ventured in. The Kenyan people were always anxious to do us little favours, in exchange for a little money, and they would some- times shimmy up a tree to bring us a coconut. They would adeptly lop off the top of the coconut, stick in a straw and pass it to us with much decorum! Coconut milk was not anything I would request on a daily basis, but the mangoes and pine- apples, which were always available, were the favourites of most everyone.

I recall having gathered with a number of other people in a large pavilion on the beach one day. An amazing band was playing and we were all enjoying the music of the band and the singers when, suddenly, the rain began to come down in torrents. The winds picked up sending blasts of water over the wall of windows that faced the ocean so that nothing outside was visible. The sounds of the storm drowned out everything, including the band. An African storm, especially one on the ocean, can be quite ferocious and unpredictable. This storm, however, petered out in a few hours and although it spoiled the mood of what had started out to be a fun-filled day, there was only minimal damage to property and no personal injuries.

Our time in Mombasa passed and we returned to Nairobi where we moved from the Hilton Hotel into a lovely country inn. There we mingled with other patrons who were in Kenya doing missionary work, mostly people from the Presbyterian and Seventh-day Adventist Churches. It seems to me that church groups and other small outfits do extraordinary work in Africa without ever getting the credit that the larger agencies like UNICEF, OXFAM, UNHCR and others receive. Of course, the churches' mission is supposed to be to serve without expecting or wanting recognition for their good deeds.

Within a few days, we received orders to return to Khartoum. I thought this would be a straightforward trip without complications of any kind. I had my reissued passport in hand and the Khartoum representative for WUSC was supposed to meet us at the airport with our entrance visas. To our great dismay, when the plane landed this official was nowhere to be found. How irresponsible was that? The Sudanese customs officer informed us that without our entrance visas, we would have to reboard the plane and go wherever it was going. A fine state of affairs this was! I've experienced, in my lifetime, what I've considered to be something akin to miracles, and now I was about to experience another. While I was imploring the Sudanese official to do something to enable us to stay, if only at the airport, until someone from WUSC could be contacted to provide the missing documents, an imposing looking uniformed gentleman appeared, shook hands with me and my wife, and stated that he knew me. He instructed the official to prepare documents for him to sign. I don't know exactly what he said as my knowledge of Arabic was very limited, but the document was prepared and signed and, with a broad smile and a handshake, he said we were free to go. I was greatly relieved, to say the least. I thanked him profusely. I don't recall ever seeing this man before, but he might have recognized me from some United Nations gathering we could have both attended. In any event, I certainly appreciated his intervention on our behalf.

By now, UNDP had constructed a new communications building, and they were gradually hiring the Sudanese personnel to fill the communications positions. I decided it was time for me to return to Canada. With thanks to TOTAL for allowing us to occupy their Sudanese personnel residence while we were in Khartoum, I closed up shop and we went home.

During the course of my Royal Canadian Air Force and External Affairs careers, my family and I had spent nearly 20 years in Ottawa, and considered that to be our home base. But, since our daughter was attending university in the United States, we decided to go back to our roots and we returned to Corner Brook. However, in my opinion, I was still too young to retire, so I decided, against my wife's wishes – what's new? – to try something different. My nephew Byron Moores and I bought a boat, a converted long liner, 44 feet long and 14 feet wide, powered by a 160 hp diesel with a capacity to carry 20 passengers, and with sleeping accommodations for six. We decided to use it as a tour boat on the Bay of Islands. We had to adhere to Canadian Coast Guard regulations, so the first things we had to do was to obtain a 25-man life raft, 25 life jackets, long-range radar, and a VHF radio. After passing the necessary inspection and obtaining our permits, Byron and I had to take a short course in order to qualify for small boat captains' tickets.

We then set about installing benches for seating, a canopy and some decorative paraphernalia. Last but not least, we had to secure the passenger loading area and docking facilities. We were advised of our distance limitation – South Head, the entrance to Bay of Islands, to Crabb's Brook on the north side of the bay. This meant we could go anywhere between these locations: Green Island, Big and French Islands, Cox's Cove, Brake's Cove and other small islands, approximately 20 in total. There were lots of glitches along the way, including the difficulty of obtaining proper advertising, financing, etc. But, finally, we were open for business.

When the weather cooperated, we had very enjoyable tours and charter trips. We stopped in selected areas and passengers were able to jig codfish, always very popular, and my nephew dove for scallops which we cooked on board and served free of charge. On charter trips, we used our galley facilities and a barbecue to cook some very tasty Newfoundland meals. Considering the short tourist season in Newfoundland, and the often inclement weather, we did extremely well for two summers. However, since Byron was a young man with a family, he felt the need to secure more stable employment and so I sold out to him and he continued to use the boat for another season to take advantage of some charter opportunities.

Well, as for us, we had had enough of Newfoundland for the time being, so back to Ottawa we go...talk about nomads! In 1990-91, the First Gulf War was in progress; Iraqi President Saddam Hussein had invaded the small country of Kuwait, Iraq's neighbour, and the United States had gone in to assist Kuwait in the ouster of its enemy. Consequently, the Canadian government set up an operation centre called EPC, Emergency Preparedness Canada, which came under the auspices of the Privy Council Office in Ottawa. I had returned at the opportune time to secure a position with this agency. Together with other Watch Officers, I monitored all worldwide traffic coming into the centre, and extracted any and all information that might be of interest and pertinent to the Canadian government. It was a fascinating job but, after a time, I terminated my employment in favour of the freedom to spend some time in the United States. My daughter and son-in-law were living in Detroit at the time and they were expecting their first child. While still maintaining our residence in Ottawa, we moved to Royal Oak, a suburb of Detroit. When our grandson, Joshua, was two, we moved further south to St. Louis, Missouri, where we lived for eight years, our home base being first in Ottawa and later on in

Sarnia, Ontario. Our final US move followed when we relocated to St. Paul, Minneapolis, with our home base becoming our newly acquired house on the West Coast of Newfoundland.

We had made many trips to the United States, and we had covered a lot of territory while Eydie was a college student in Kentucky and Detroit. After my retirement, we had the opportunity to travel to many places that piqued our interests: much of the Western States of Colorado, Montana and Wyoming, and in the East, our most favourite place, Washington, DC, in cherry blossom time, and Cape Hatteras in North Carolina. With advancing age and its associated health issues, and with the interjection of a little common sense, we have finally become weary of travelling and now spend most of our time in Newfoundland, the best place of all. Although we miss certain benefits associated with living in highly populated areas, we certainly do not crave the hustle and bustle that goes along with it, nor the criminal activity that seems endemic to most large cities. It is sad to note, however, that such activity is fast becoming a fact of life even in some of the smaller out-of-the-way places in Newfoundland.

As for the inclement weather that we do so much complaining about, and we do get more than our share, we are still privileged to have the changing seasons, far superior to what we have experienced in many other places, including the US, which endured the disastrous Great Flood in St. Louis, Missouri, while we were there in 1993. Our daughter and her husband headed up a group from the Salvation Army, and they operated canteens, provided other necessary support services, and did everything they could to help people with their various problems. They worked in conjunction with the American Red

Cross and the United States Coast Guard. Eydie often went with the Coast Guard to help in persuading people to leave their homes; many were incapable of evacuating themselves, others didn't want to leave their animals, and for this and many other personal reasons they needed some gentle coaxing. In the end, houses were moved off their foundations and washed away when the levees broke, and throughout the massive flooding there was a tremendous loss of homes, farms, and business properties, and 50 people were killed. We explored the area when the flood waters finally started to subside in August, and to see church steeples barely peaking up through the water, service stations with their gas tanks completely submerged, farmlands underwater with their silos swept off their foundations and destroyed; everywhere, such ruin was horrendous. People are amazingly resilient in situations such as this but, most assuredly, there were times when they felt that the obstacles facing them made the possibility of rebuilding their lives seem hopeless and insurmountable.

Not only was there massive flooding in St. Louis, but many times during tornado season, we found it necessary to take refuge in the basement in response to the warning sirens going off. In Minnesota, a tornado swept the entire mile-long street on which we lived, knocking out transformers, lifting the roofs off houses, destroying property, and uprooting 100-year old-trees. We lived at the intersection of two main streets and, perhaps because of our location, we got through the frightening experience almost unscathed. Kentucky showed us some serious flooding where tobacco crops were wiped out, and Cape Hatturas presented its own version of an out-of-control storm. All in all, it's rather comforting to be away from it all and to be in Newfoundland where our worst weather consists of snow, rain and fog.

EPILOGUE

Although I grew up in Newfoundland in the 1930s and 40s, and the Newfoundland I knew then is dramatically different from what it is today, it is a source of satisfaction to me that I have been able to return to my roots. Like most Newfoundlanders, I have come to appreciate the many positive changes that have taken place in this province over the years, especially since the advent of Confederation with Canada in 1949: education, libraries, recreational and cultural facilities, and health care.

Even more significant is the emergence of the computer age with its associated benefits of the internet, email, iPhones, Skype, etc. It is now relatively easy to make contacts in just about every part of the world. Just recently my teenage grandson Joshua went on a mission, with his church group, to Ghana in East Africa. While he was there, he became quite ill and could not be evacuated to his home in the United States; this was the time when European airports were shut down because much of the country was blanketed with ash from the erupting Icelandic volcano. Joshua's parents were able to be in constant contact with the hospital and doctors by iPhone, and they with us, his grandparents, who were able to talk with Joshua and to see him by way of Skype. Contrast this with the young Newfoundland husbands, sons and brothers who went off to serve in World Wars I and II. It was as if they had stepped out into the darkness and disappeared.

Aside from better health care, since Confederation seniors have more financial security than ever before and, for whatever reason, they are living longer lives and seem to be enjoying themselves more…since I am only 90, I'll have to wait until I'm old to be able to either affirm or deny this assumption! In any event, it is gratifying to see our province progress from a "have not" to a "have" province with incredible assets. It only took us the best part of 500 years.

I expect I have to consider myself retired. Looking back, I can say I have had a great life and, even if it were possible, there isn't much I would have done differently. My re-enlisting in the military (Peacetime RCAF Branch) was a positive move. My chosen trade of communications could have had me sent to such places as Frobisher Bay, classified as hardship postings, but instead I was privileged to go to some choice postings like Goose Bay, Trenton, Ottawa and overseas. Fort Churchill did not fit into that category because it was such a harsh environment, and it was particularly difficult for my wife who was still recuperating from two major surgeries and a month's worth of radiation treatment; her being alone so much when I had to be away on assignments was difficult for her. However, even Fort

Churchill was an interesting experience and both of us are happy that we were able to complete our two-year stint there. In the military, you go where you are needed according to your trade, and you learn to deal with any negatives that present themselves, like moving a dozen times in as many years. We were privileged to be able to travel extensively, and I am happy we did it early in life because, at this stage, travelling to St. John's or even to Corner Brook sometimes seems like a major undertaking. I must say that to have been a part of the military Trumpet and Drum Band at various posts, and of the Pipe and Drum Band with its travel around Europe, were some of the highlights of my life. As an added bonus, I had the opportunity to play music for entertainment at all of my postings…the extra money I was able to earn was a big plus for me!

My years on various oil rigs presented some harrowing experiences, especially since I was 60 when I took on this new career. The training exercises performed in the mouth of Freshwater Bay were a challenge in themselves. One February, we were in and out of the Bay's frigid waters testing rafts and newly acquired survival suits. The swimming pool at Memorial University was where we practiced escaping from a submerged helicopter cabin while upside down in the water. We were allotted just 11 seconds in which to escape and return to the surface – not an easy feat for me without the benefit of my eyeglasses and with my considerable girth. My fellow crewmen were always supportive of the old guy in our more difficult maneuvers, and I am sure I provided them with the scattered bit of "comic relief." One of our more difficult tests, at least for me, was the Fire Fighting Course sanctioned by the Safety Board. However, I managed to survive this as well, only to take on the dangers of the *Ocean Ranger* and of the *John Shaw*. One of the things I most disliked about the oil rigs was the time-consuming travel from wherever the rig was located back and forth to my home in Ottawa. I did manage to be available for many of the events important to my daughter but there were some things which I regret having missed.

As for Africa, the mission of the United Nations in Sudan was to provide food, through the World Food Program, to the thousands of people who would otherwise have starved. I believe that, like myself, the majority of people who go on missions to Africa, and to many other such troubled places, do so out of a desire to be a part of something that matters. In Sudan, my wife and I were fortunate to have had comfortable living accommodations although my wife was less than thrilled with the lizard(s) that often performed their exercises on our bedroom wall, or slithered out from underneath the refrigerator or the washing machine. Contending with the extreme heat was stressful, and the *haboobs* left sand and grit everywhere no matter how snug the doors and windows. When I travelled to outposts like El Fasher, El Geneina, Juba or Fort St. John, living conditions were somewhat crude but adequate for my needs. I didn't need or expect anything more. We were always deeply appreciative of the fact that, due to the generosity of the British, we were able to take advantage of their amenities, their store, their club, swimming pool, and library when we were in Khartoum. My wife particularly made good use of the library as she spent so much time alone and could not go outside. She could go up on the roof, for a change of scenery, providing she went up before 7:00 a.m. or after 9:00 or 10:00 p.m.; I'm sure her days often seemed endless.

After Africa I was contacted by the International Branch of the Salvation Army, and on another occasion by the Catholic Mercy Corps about serving on overseas missions. Either of these I would have been honoured to accept. However, because of my age, the necessary documentation, including medical insurance, could not be processed, and I was unable to take advantage of the opportunity. Since I was not yet ready to fully retire, I took up, or reactivated, a few other interests like speaking to various groups – Rotary Clubs, Senior Citizens, Veterans, and in schools, both in the United States and Canada. Now I only occasionally speak to students, but I do go and play a few tunes on the organ for the "Old Folks" who are something of a captive audience. The classic song, "Maggie," by Foster and Allen which begins, "I wandered today to the hills, Maggie, to watch the scene below," includes the verse,

> They say I am feeble with age, Maggie
> My steps are much slower than then
> My face is a well-written page, Maggie
> And time all alone was the pen

This particular verse describes me well, and I am trying to stay alive and be as active as possible. As my brother-in-law, Frank Moores, says, "The best way to do that is to keep on breathing as long as you can."

So-o-o, I'll do that!

ACKNOWLEDGEMENTS

I would like to thank Bess Dyke, Hazel (Dyke) Clarke, Eydie Dyke Shypulski, and especially my wife, Ruby, without whose support and efforts this manuscript would not have been possible. I would also like to thank my good RCAF friend, W/O Bob-Ross, bagpiper extraordinaire, for his loyal support and encouragement.